MODERN WEST

MODERN WEST

CHASE REYNOLDS EWALD

PHOTOGRAPHS BY AUDREY HALL

Gibbs Smith

CONTENTS

INTRODUCTION

For more than three decades as a photographer-writer team, we have documented the ever-evolving landscape of architecture and interior design in the American West. We've watched trends shift and styles redefine themselves, even within the realms of rustic and modern Western architecture. Because of this immersion, we recognize when it's time to revisit a genre and a particular way of living. *Modern West* is that look.

In *Modern West*, we continue our exploration of design and architecture in the region, selecting homes that aren't just modern for modernity's sake. While some are striking and lavish—ski-slope retreats, ranch compounds, and a beautifully executed, classically modern Teton Valley home—each remains a unique expression of how people choose to live in the contemporary West.

Throughout the region, there's a continuous pendulum swing between traditional rustic and modern rustic design. While "mountain modern" has become an overused phrase, it remains useful in capturing a style defined by contemporary sensibilities and regional authenticity in both form and material. There is an emphasis on the interplay between structure and landscape, blurring the boundaries between indoors and outdoors. The best work achieves a careful balance—between ruggedness and refinement, scale and subtlety, tradition and innovation.

The homes in *Modern West* vary widely, reflecting the diversity of Western living. A dream home in the West now means different things to different people. Some seek a sense of belonging—to landscape, community, or history. Others prioritize a curated, individual aesthetic over a nostalgic Western ideal. These homeowners are not necessarily pursuing the classical romantic vision.

Rather, they're expressing an individualized aesthetic, bringing together the many influences that shape their lives: their art and belongings, their personal histories, travels and collections. While the West is experiencing a cultural and demographic shift, accelerated by remote work and an influx of new residents, a younger generation, drawn to the region's landscapes and opportunities, is also redefining what home means here. For them, modern Western living isn't necessarily about a mountainside ski house for family holiday gatherings or a remote rustic cabin, but about creating a life—one that integrates their work, passions, and connection to place in a way that feels both deeply personal and undeniably Western. Whether minimalist or eclectic, these homes are distinctly modern while unquestionably rooted in place.

As the region evolves, so do the challenges that come with growth: water, fire, land use, and the increasing tension between preservation and progress. Thoughtful design is no longer just a matter of aesthetics; it's a necessity. These homes are more than showcases of style. They are considered responses to site, lifestyle, and the shifting realities of living and working in the contemporary West.

Modernism here is not a singular aesthetic but a broad and evolving spectrum, spanning historic renovations, bold contemporary builds, and everything in between. What unites them is a deep respect for the landscape, a pursuit of authenticity, and an understanding that a home in the West is not just about where you live, but how you choose to live.

—Chase Reynolds Ewald and Audrey Hall

SHOULDER SEASON

SHOULDER SEASON

The house was enormous, and heavy, a panoply of massive logs resting atop oversized stone piers, a statement-making porte cochere, and lots of gables and rooflines punctuated by dormers. Inside, volumes were immense, especially in the great room with its double-height river rock fireplace and phalanx of exposed trusses, and in the kitchen, a symphony of wood. Today the home has been transformed: the exterior simplified with wood lap siding and standing-seam metal roofs, rounded river rocks replaced with clean-edge Montana moss rock, the interior opened up with vaulted steel trusses, steel columns, and steel-and-glass window walls. Even more impactful was the reorientation of the layout. Now, dual axes create a central sight line to the Wasatch Mountains, establishing a strong sense of place from the moment of entry.

When Greg and Karen Conway first viewed the home, they had difficulty seeing past this robust expression of 1990s log living. They'd been overseas for twenty-four years, but had always returned to mountain towns, eventually settling on Park City. Now they were seeking a forever home, and, despite its dated presentation, this was a special opportunity.

"This was the lot the developer kept," explains Greg. "It's at the end of the road and backs onto the ski mountain. No one skis by our windows, but we can walk out to a lift and are frequently the first on it. A lot of the homes of this size and quality are higher up and cut into the mountain, which means the south-facing exposure tends to be the garage. Our house is on a flat lot, the back yard is big and faces south, and we're only a few minutes from the highway.

That combination of factors led us to buy a house we didn't really like."

To tackle the structure's aesthetics, flow, and livability, the Conways brought in JLF Architects and their design-build partner Big-D Signature. Verdone Landscape Architects crafted outdoor amenities, including two firepits, multiple outdoor "rooms," and a pool tucked behind a low wall with a water feature. The first task, according to architect Jake Scott, was to "right size" the house. "The house had a lot of really heavy architecture: massive columns and a really big entry, and there wasn't much openness to the outside. It needed to be lightened up. The other thing was, as their retirement place, this was bigger than they'd need when it was just two of them. That was a challenge because with a big log stairway and thirty-inch columns, it had this massive mountain-home feel that didn't fit their personalities. The question became, how do we bring more timelessness of character, and how do we make it more comfortable for two people?"

They started by playing up the sunlit back side of the house, flipping the kitchen and dining room north to south, which allows the Conways to entertain directly from dining room to terrace, adding windows on each side of the building and aligning the firepit near the entry on the open line through the house and across the back terrace to end at the water feature wall, creating a visual line straight through the house. With the interiors opened up to draw the light, connect to the outdoors, and celebrate views, they moved on to more practical considerations. A bedroom off the kitchen became a family room, with Karen's office adjacent. The kitchen is

There are times when you really can't understand the significance of the "after" without having a grasp of the "before."

now bright white and open to the outdoors; the dining room given separation-with-transparency with a glass partition. The primary bath's eighteen-foot vaulted ceiling was made flat while two upstairs bedrooms became three. The basement now houses a bunk room, gym, table tennis, bar area, and wine room. Barnwood ceilings throughout create coziness in smaller rooms and foster a feeling of intimacy within larger oak-floored volumes.

London-based designer Debra McQuin and local designer Robyn Seldin worked on the interiors, a mix of new and custom furnishings and pieces from the Conways' London home. Christian Liaigre sofas, mid-century-modern Brazilian chairs, and classic Knoll and vintage Danish modern pieces are combined with interesting fabrics, wallpapers, and drapes to soften hard surfaces. The extensive art collection includes works by Henry Moore, Margo Hoff and Navajo painter Patrick Dean Hubbell, and photography by William Klein, Saul Leiter, Henri Cartier-Bresson, and Doug and Mike Starn, as well as Malian artist Malick Sidibe' and Finnish photographer Ola Kolehmainen.

The changes have been transformative, says Karen. "When we moved here full time, we were empty nesters; ninety percent of the time it's just two people and a dog. But we wanted a space where, when our kids come back, there would be room for everybody. The architects transformed the exterior, then put glass and steel through the center of house so you can see from front to back. They turned a house that was clunky, dark, and overbearing into one that's welcoming."

The log mansion was very much a product of its time. This new iteration—light-filled, outdoors-embracing—was the perfect landing spot for well-traveled expats who finally came home.

A dark and dated log home of immense volumes was remarkably transformed into a light-filled home infused with art and color by JLF Architects, Big-D Signature, Verdone Landscape Architects, and interior designers Debra McQuin and Robyn Seldin. In the soaring great room, heavy ceiling timbers were replaced by sleek steel trusses while the river rock fireplace was transformed with Montana moss rock.

The white cabinetry of the kitchen—the ultimate in light and bright—is warmed up with a reclaimed wood ceiling. The black-and-white photo *Queen Charlotte's Ball* by French master photographer Henri Cartier-Bresson offers a sense of formality and distance that contrast nicely with the intimacy of the kitchen.

RIGHT: A glass entry looks out onto naturalistic landscape designed by Verdone Landscape Architects.

OPPOSITE: With the doors flung open to greet the morning, breakfasters can enjoy the sound of water. The Platner table and Danish rosewood chairs are minimal pieces that keep the focus on the outdoors.

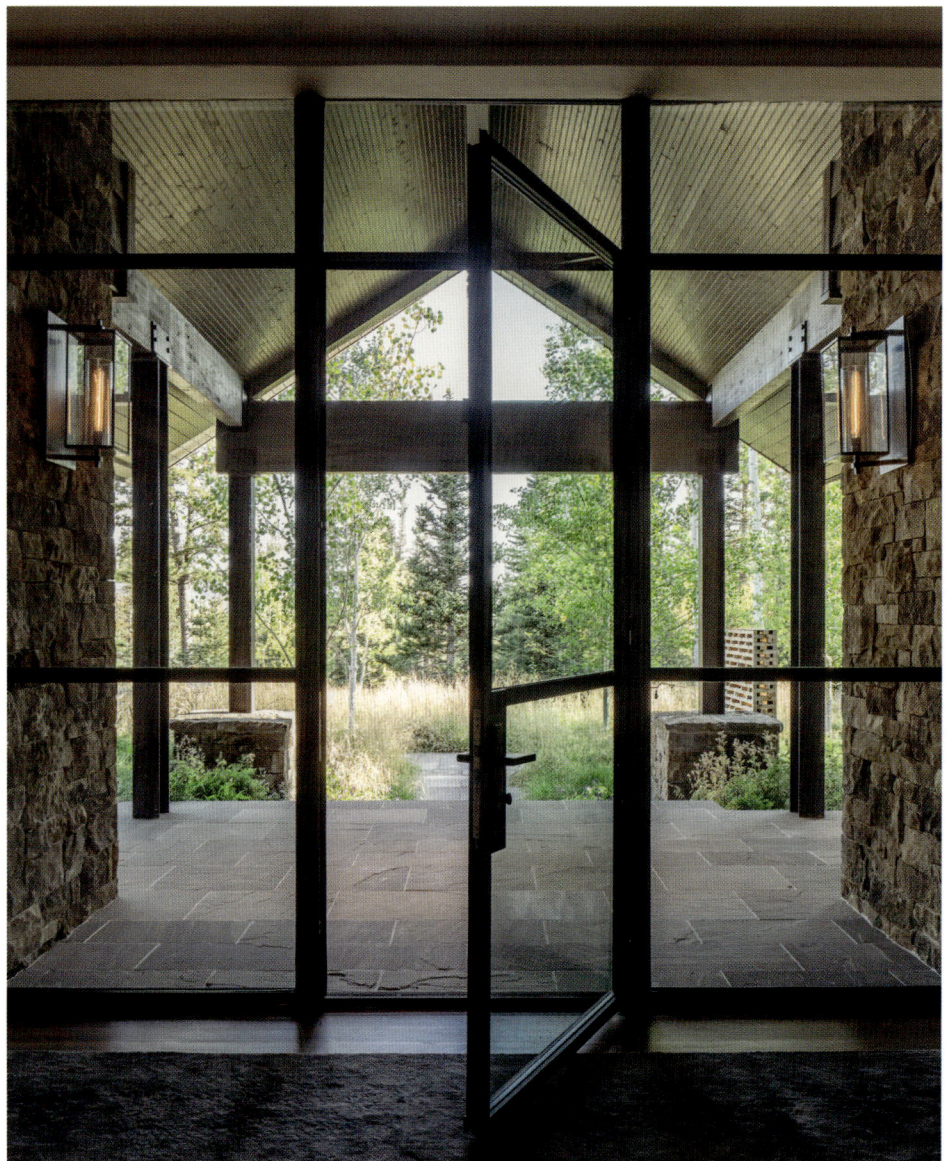

The owners' bedroom enjoys warmth, coziness, and easy access to the outdoors. And, of course, art: over the bed, a painting by Patrick Dean Hubbell, an artist who grew up in the Navajo nation and graduated from the School at the Art Institute of Chicago. The cross motif features in much of his work. Twin brothers Doug and Mike Starn created the photo collage over the fireplace.

The primary bathroom is a study in "less is more," says homeowner Greg Conway. "It had previously been much larger, with a double-height ceiling and an intricately carved wood mantel surrounding a fireplace. The design focus here, as in much of the renovations, was a process of taking away and simplifying." The black-and-white photo above the Iris cast-iron vessel tub is by Stephen Inggs, a professor of printmaking in Cape Town. The floors and counters are Taj Mahal stone; the Rousseau chandeliers are from Hudson Valley Lighting.

WHITE SNOW,
BLACK DIAMONDS

WHITE SNOW,
BLACK DIAMONDS

For a longtime Yellowstone Club family, the opportunity to move to a newly developed part of the resort coupled with the chance to design a new home from a blank canvas proved irresistible. The fact that the just-under-construction townhouse also enjoyed ski-in ski-out access made the decision that much simpler.

The site benefited from the enormous vistas that give Big Sky its name. Lone Mountain towers to the northwest, and expansive views span the village core and main lodge to the distinctive shape of Andesite. Because of those views and the steep slope, the placement of the new structures was self-evident, says Locati Architects' Corey Kelly. "We had no option because of the way the hillside faces and the way the house is platted on the contour of the mountain slope. But that was fine because the view is spectacular." Also, he adds, "This lot is very steep, which was advantageous for this design."

Enter New York-based designer John Vancheri, who had worked with the homeowners on several projects over the course of a decade, including at the Yellowstone Club. For the designer, the rustic modern exterior of stone, wood, and timber mandated by the club served as a challenge to create distinctive, dramatic interiors that blur the line between rustic modern and simply modern. In Big Sky, he explains, "My first project at the Yellowstone Club was for this same family four years prior. At the time, the typical aesthetic seen at the club was more traditional; it had a rustic Western feel with antlers, plaid, heavy timbers, and fieldstone. I wanted to make that space more modern while keeping it rustic using indigenous woods and stone, creating an open floor plan and adding modern

furniture. For this new project, I wanted to push the look even further, making it more sleek. Instead of the rustic elements, I brought in steel, glass, metal details and cleaner stone choices, in addition to an open plan and modern furniture."

The views have an enormous impact from each of the key spaces in the house. Vancheri anchored the interiors against that limitless sky with a blend of steel, black elements, and reclaimed timber. Central to the design is the fireplace, a structural marvel open on three sides, its suspended chimney portion a modernist artwork of black steel grated panels, their lines running vertically, horizontally, and diagonally, delivering an injection of energy. The fireplace creates dialogue with the staircase, which Vancheri designed in steel with wood treads in tones of light gray matching the floor and a steel mesh railing. A custom thirty-foot-tall light fixture spans the entire height of the building, from the third-floor ceiling to the rec room floor. Glass walls help delineate interior spaces at each level while maintaining the flow of light and a sense of airiness.

The designer created drawings for everything from the interior layout (he opened the spaces to the views and sacrificed some deck square footage for interior living) and cabinetry to custom furniture and built-ins, custom lighting and many pieces of furniture. He also specified extraordinarily tall door openings, where possible, to enhance the feeling of openness and passage of light.

Guests enter on the main level into the great room, which opens to the dining room, which in turn opens to the kitchen. There, a cozy breakfast nook creates its own semi-separate space; a catering kitchen tucked

The views have an enormous impact from each of the key spaces in the house. Vancheri anchored the interiors against that limitless sky with a blend of steel, black elements, and reclaimed timber.

out of sight allows for easy entertaining. This level also accommodates the primary suite, a mudroom, and outdoor living. The centrally located staircase provides access to an upper level, which hosts three guest bedrooms, and the lower floor, which consists of a guest suite and a four-queen bunkroom, laundry, a wine vault with glass-and-steel doors, and a sauna. A game room with a bar—which, thanks to the steep slope of the lot, also enjoys spectacular views—opens out to a hot tub on a raised deck for a full entertaining program.

The interior palette at first glance reads as black-and-white, but any feeling of starkness is alleviated throughout the rooms by creamy plaster walls, splashes of dark green in the fabrics, and gray tones in the floor. Says the designer, "The color scheme was inspired by the outdoors, the winter snow whites, and the evergreen blacks and greens."

The main living space combines highly figured countertops and a sleek metal hood in the kitchen with a dark wood table, black chairs with cozy sheepskin seats and backs, and minimal pendant lighting in the dining area. In the living room, inviting seating in dark mossy green is oriented toward the dramatic views, where an upholstered bench suspended in front of the view window creates a near focal point and punctuates the floor-to-ceiling glazing. The room is finished with rectilinear white stone coffee tables, bold artwork, and a textural rug, all of which serve to further the contrasting dark/light aesthetic.

The expansiveness is balanced by moments of intimacy. In the great room, a bench connected to the hearth creates a cozy vignette for a chess table made of the same leathered black granite as the hearth. A moody windowless powder room is a study in minimalism. Vancheri employed texture to define spaces and create spaces within spaces, such as in the dining area, where he designed a fifteen-foot-long wood top with a zigzag pattern and placed it atop two round pedestals. The primary bedroom goes decidedly glam with a headboard wall and built-in bed of charmeuse velvet with gold highlights, while the serene primary suite bath is softened with heavy flannel off-white drapes. "The richness warms up the more monochromatic spaces," Vancheri explains.

Throughout the home, furniture with rounded shapes—the custom sofa in the rec room, wooly ottomans, the console table in the entry, and various small tables—provides contrast to minimal pieces with sharply defined edges. This is a home that celebrates contrast between dark and light, interior and exterior, hard and soft, industrial and domestic, immediate and afar. Those contrasts pump up the intrigue and energy of the home, providing the perfect counterpoint to the ever-present drama outside the windows.

Homes at the Yellowstone Club feature extraordinary views of Lone Mountain. This residence—designed by New York-based designer John Vancheri with Locati Architects and Schlauch Bottcher Construction—plays on the drama of the views with floor-to-ceiling windows and a palette of strong contrasts. In the great room, Vancheri combined Holly Hunt chandeliers with an OKHA armchair in a plush bouclé from Castel and Poliform sofas in velvet. The blackened steel hanging swing in front of the windows is custom by John Vancheri Interior Design, with fabric from Designtex. The rug from Woven continues the black-and-white palette.

PRECEDING OVERLEAF:
Natural light floods the kitchen and breakfast banquette/hangout area, which offer views directly onto the ski slopes and gondola. The room features a GUBI table, Suite NY chairs, and a ceiling fixture from Holly Hunt. Pale white oak floors lighten the space. The custom hood by John Vancheri Interior Design has a blackened steel finish; the countertops are coastal gray Caesarstone.

RIGHT: A large rec room for grown-ups with game table, seating, media, and a billiards table adjoins a wine room separated by a sleek glass-and-steel door. The minimal pendant is from Workstead. The banquette with curved sofa is custom by John Vancheri Interior Design, covered in a bouclé from Knoll.

OVERLEAF, LEFT: A serene guest bedroom looks out onto a snow-covered hillside.

OVERLEAF, RIGHT:
Liminal spaces around the staircase have glass walls that bounce light and add interest. Vancheri added texture through stools from Cuff Studio upholstered in a bouclé from Pierre Frey and an area rug from Marc Phillips.

CALATRAVA

ZAHA HADID

OPPOSITE: A custom fabricated bed by John Vancheri Interior Design covered in Maharam velvet anchors the primary bedroom. Mohair benches and a Tibetano rug makes it cozy. Throughout the house, ceiling beams and doorframes were made from reclaimed timber sources from old industrial buildings; painted black, they still show their history through holes and notches.

LEFT: Designer John Vancheri designed the contemporary railings and staircase—light-colored wood treads rest atop one blackened steel stringer, making them appear to float. Vancheri also chose the contemporary light fixture from The Future Perfect that runs through the entire structure.

WYOMING BASE CAMP

WYOMING BASE CAMP

For a Texas resident who had a long history in Jackson Hole—he'd even ski bummed there for a time in his youth—the longing to have a place to hang his own hat was as persistent as his love of the Tetons. And because downhill skiing was a driving force behind the yearning for a second home, the Shooting Star community, with its proximity to the ski mountain, was a natural choice. However, the site was constrained by both neighboring homes and a stream, not to mention the homeowners' association's strictures on roof pitches and lengths. The project was made more complex by the husband's love of modernism and the wife's preference for a more traditional aesthetic.

The client had an acquaintance with the founder of CLB Architects that stretched back many years; he admired the firm's take on mountain modernism, especially its ability to find new and creative ways to express the forms and materials of Western vernacular architecture. CLB Principal Sam Ankeny, who grew up in Jackson and was uniquely positioned to navigate the sometimes-competing considerations of the project, imagined a design that would achieve a unique expression in traditional forms with a contemporary energy, all while maximizing views and minimizing the impact of neighboring properties.

The house is in stained cedar, charcoal quartzite, and patinaed copper with a shingle roof. It presents as three gabled forms staggered to view, surrounded by low stacked-stone walls and planters with aspens, backed by mountains rising precipitously behind. Roofs constructed with cross-laminated timbers allowed large overhangs (up to seven feet on the larger buildings)

in both directions. The closest and largest volume accommodates the garage on the near side and three guest rooms above, with the kitchen and a screened porch extending toward the mountains. To the left, the lowest volume contains the primary bedroom, office, and junior suite. Rather than linking the volumes with glass hallways, low connecting elements house distinct functions: the dining room on one side, an intimate den on the other.

The central volume is differentiated by its material treatment. It lies at the terminus of a wide walkway in a small courtyard, a symmetrical peaked form clad in stone. The custom wood door is set between glass panels, which, with additional glazing above the steel-detailed transom, creates a lantern effect at night that guides arrivals to the entry. Upon crossing the threshold, visitors enter into the most formal moment of the home. There they are struck by the full impact of the view. The sightline is centered on Rendezvous Mountain, while the peak of the ceiling—wood-lined and supported by wood trusses with steel details—echoes the distinct shape of the peak etched against the sky. With stone walls extending seamlessly past the windows to create a sheltered outdoor room, the effect is a euphoric celebration of place.

The home's interiors establish a rugged yet refined aesthetic through a combination of stone and richly toned wood. Copper panels, accenting the low connective sections of the house, are brought inside—in the paneled fireplace in the den and the range hood above the kitchen island. Walnut, a strong preference of the husband's, is seen in cabinetry, floors, doors, and

The home's interiors establish a rugged yet refined aesthetic through a combination of stone and richly toned wood.

millwork. It also appears on walls, such as in the wood volume that defines the cozy den; in places, it runs from floor to wall to ceiling carve-outs. In the powder room, ebonized walnut, slightly darker than in the rest of the house, creates a distinct and edgy mood.

When it came to furnishings, explains CLB Interiors' Maria James, "The husband wanted a modern house stylistically, but the wife likes a more traditional vibe, so the forms are traditional but with clean lines. To alleviate those hard lines, we introduced curves in furnishings and used some softened materials and wall coverings. There are a lot of curves and a lot of sculptural qualities, like in tabletops. The wife didn't want a lot of color, but she liked the idea of mixing up textural feels, so we introduced very light colors, subtle patterns, and comfortable soft fabrics. She also loved glass chandeliers, so we tried to find pieces that were a little more modern in form. We were trying to push her a little out of her comfort zone but also respect what she loved. It was a good collaborative effort."

Ultimately, notes Ankeny, the main driver of the project, beyond a passion for Jackson Hole, was creating a place to bring people together. "Family was such an important part of this project," he says. "The owners have three daughters and some grandkids. They're not super formal, so other than the formal moment at the entry, everything is about family coming together. The wife is a chef who grew up in Mexico and cooking is a big part of her family tradition. It's the kitchen that's the center of activity."

These days, when the builders or architects stop by for a visit, they inevitably are invited to sit down to enjoy handmade tamales with their clients-now-friends. It's then that they have the satisfaction of seeing multiple generations making the highest and best use of this unique home in the shadow of the Tetons.

A Jackson, Wyoming, home designed by CLB Architects balances traditional and modern aesthetics to satisfy the contrasting preferences of the homeowners. In the living room, Mimi London's Three Timber table, the Belgard Daybed from Dmitriy & Co., and Wisp nesting tables from OCHRE are backed by the warm glow of a custom copper-paneled fireplace surround.

Bob Langrish's WORLD OF HORSES

Anouk Kramm WILD HORSES OF CUMBERLAND ISLAND

THE WILD HORSES OF SABLE ISLAND
Roberto Dutesco

The exterior is of charcoal quartzite stone, resawn cedar, and patinaed copper panels with exaggerated overhangs that emphasize the gable roof forms and create protection from the elements. The materials are applied differently on each of the home's three primary gables, which ascend from a one-story master wing to a one-and-a-half-story living space to a two-story guest wing that houses the garage.

OPPOSITE: In the dining room, CLB's interiors department, led by Maria James, combined a custom Lorraine refectory table from Gregorius Pineo with A. Rudin dining chairs in leather and velvet and a Noor rug from STARK. The Ostrea chandelier is from John Pomp.

LEFT: The O'Neal bench from Highland House creates a focal point at the end of a hallway where volumes are delineated with stone and wood treatment.

LEFT: A custom copper hood in the kitchen brings exterior materials inside. Walnut cabinetry creates consistency throughout the house as does the Town Studio counter stools from A. Rudin in a walnut finish.

OVERLEAF, LEFT: In the kitchen's intimate dining nook, Laced Rawhide armless chairs by McGuire add a hint of rustic to the more contemporary treatments, such as Knoll's Saarinen dining table. The sconces are from John Brooks.

OVERLEAF, RIGHT: The wall treatment in the moody powder room is amplified by the burnished tones of the hammered copper bowl.

OFF-PISTE
SUN VALLEY

OFF-PISTE SUN VALLEY

Architect Peter Zimmerman is a Pennsylvania-based designer who loves the challenge inherent in designing site-specific mountain homes. When new clients, a Pennsylvania family of five who lived in a traditional stone farmhouse, approached him about the lot they had purchased on a mountainside in Sun Valley, he recalls, "I said to them, 'Good architecture is not the clothes you put on the architecture—whether it's a Pennsylvania farmhouse, a house in Florida, or a log house in Jackson. It's much more about the inherent aspects: proportion, scale, harmony, shadow, and light.'"

The house he designed with project architect Sean Narcum incorporates all those architectural principles while making the best use of its dramatic site. Tucked into the landscape, the wood, stone, glass, and metal structure reveals itself by degrees. The first glimpse upon approach takes in a long cantilevered roof and prominent gable housing a lantern-like glass entrance. In the foreground, the naturalistic landscape is studded with sage and grasses; behind the structure, Bald Mountain rises vertiginously, reminding the viewer of architecture's proper place on the edge of the Western wilderness.

And Sun Valley, for all its sybaritic pleasures, does perch on the edge of wilderness, the largest contiguous swath of undeveloped lands in the lower forty-eight. It's only fitting that new structures defer to nature. This home—with construction by Lee Gilman Builders, interiors by Barbara Gisel Design, and landscapes by BYLA Landscape Architects—achieves this, with the main volume maintaining a low profile from the road but expanding to a lower story as the ground falls away to the north. The taller gabled form speaks to the surrounding mountainscape, both in materials and its alignment to the primary view and two upthrusting stone chimneys.

With the home's horizontal lines downplaying the impact of the lived experience, visitors are well-positioned for a big reveal. "In front, the architecture is solid," explains Zimmerman, "but as you move through, it begins to explode and becomes all about the experience of the site. In the front, it's about contextually slipping into the landscape; in the back, it's about engaging in the big view."

At the entrance, the effect is striking. Transparency from front to back draws the eye straight through the heart of the home to the vast open expanse beyond, with awe-inducing views of Bald Mountain, Dollar Mountain, and the Smokey Mountain Range. To the south, the flat-roofed portion extends west to a living space, whose walls open on two sides, then dramatically cantilevers out to create protected outdoor living spaces that cascade down the hillside in multiple levels. A long, gabled form with a light-filled hallway extends north to private areas. The home's glass-walled rear elevation is centered on a contemporary staircase that descends to a family living room, three bedrooms, a gym, sauna, and steam room; it also provides outdoor access to a hot tub and firepit.

Interior spaces are defined by oak floors, fir beams, and steel-framed floor-to-ceiling windows. The open-plan living area is enhanced by wood-soffited dropped ceilings in the dining room and kitchen. Transparent light fixtures are offset with color-infused art pieces in key transitional spaces. Designer Barbara Gisel worked to keep the main spaces calm, befitting the hugely impactful views. "The clients wanted contemporary architecture with a transitional interior. They wanted it warm and cozy

"Good architecture is not the clothes you put on the architecture. . . . It's much more about the inherent aspects: proportion, scale, harmony, shadow, and light."

with a lot of personality and with art playing an important role. It was fun for us because I always think a mixture of everything makes for the best design and is also the most interesting. Bringing in nature through the art and the windows was what we played toward, plus bringing in natural elements, such as the moose horn stool and the crocodile bar, and cowboy artifacts and elements of the West that bring you back to the old times. The furniture is more modern and very neutral, augmented with splashes of colors. The art and the textures in fabrics, stone, metal, and wood all relate to each other."

Throughout the home, the rooms express drama in more intimate moments: in the steel-and-wood staircase, blue-walled office, and wood-topped bar with smoky mirrors and alligator-hide drawer fronts. A moody powder room has wallpaper of silvery aspens in a wintry state of leaflessness. In the primary bathroom, the shower walls and ceiling are lined with whitewashed, small-scale river rocks; the rectilinear white vessel tub is positioned to look directly into the treetops, creating the feel of a forest aerie.

The project has been so successful that the owners now live there full time, enjoying their place on the mountainside as it blends into its setting in all seasons. Ultimately, says Zimmerman, "All the classical traditions in architecture are very present in this house and blending with the site was critical to our approach. The success of this project, from the interior, landscape, and architectural points of view, came from clients who had opinions but were really open and engaged in the design process. They really appreciated the sense of the home relating to its environment, and they loved creating something entirely different from their previous home."

Peter Zimmerman Architects, Barbara Gisel Design, Lee Gilman Builders, and BYLA Landscape Architects designed a home well suited to its dramatic site in Sun Valley. The glass-enclosed dining room with a PELLE Designs bubble chandelier seems to float in the natural environment.

The living room features glass doors that slide open on two sides to extend the living space onto the deck, where Sun Valley's ski runs seem almost within reach. A neutral design scheme is given color, pattern, and nods to nature through textiles, including a custom bench from Berman Rosetti upholstered in hair-on leather hide. The suspended iron coffee tables are custom from Formations.

PRECEDING OVERLEAF, LEFT: Not all the spaces of the home are externally focused. In the bar, leather-fronted cabinets, glass shelves, and cool mirrored glass highlight the collections of glassware and spirits. The drawers are wrapped in caiman and elk leather by Garrett Leather.

PRECEDING OVERLEAF, RIGHT: A cozy, color-infused library treats a weaving as art. The Yerra silver shearling area rug is from Stacy Logan; the desk was custom-made by a local woodworker.

RIGHT: A mix of elements in the kitchen include the wenge-topped island, white-oak cabinetry, and a Pannelli marble backsplash. The Emile bar and counter stools from Zele Company are leather.

OFF-PISTE SUN VALLEY 63

MOUNTAIN MODERN

MOUNTAIN MODERN

A mountainside home that seems a perfect fit for its place may have a sense of inevitability about it now but it was a long time in the making.

The homeowners had spent a decade vacationing in Jackson Hole. When they realized they were ready to own a forever home, they visited mountain towns all around the Greater Yellowstone area, searching for just the right property. They'd never considered Red Lodge until a friend waxed poetic about its attributes: great skiing, a vibrant town with historic buildings and good restaurants, proximity to Yellowstone and, best of all, an off-the-beaten-path vibe. But even after buying the property, they didn't start a project right away. They waited, and they acquired more land until they had just the right configuration for building. "The final piece we bought was key," says the husband. "We built the house on that piece to face the rest of the property we'd bought earlier then we nestled it back into the mountain to make it disappear."

The clients envisioned a clean mountain look with large expanses of glass warmed up by rustic materials. By the time they designed the house, the wife laughs, "We'd had fifteen years to think about what we wanted." They chose Pearson Design Group to conceptualize the structure, OSM Construction to build it, and Field Studio landscape architects to help integrate it into the landscape. What's striking about the home, other than its siting—anchored into and embraced by the mountain, yet offering its residents an edge-of-the-precipice exhilaration—is its appropriateness. At 4,800 square feet, with a material palette of regional stone and natural weathered wood, it is human-scaled and keeps its focus on the outdoors.

"There's an inherent challenge in building on a mountain and not skylining a project," notes architect Justin Tollefson. "The house wraps to the hillside, and, especially when viewed from downhill, it blends into the hillside and the topography with the rock outcroppings. The driver for us was to make it a dynamic modern piece of architecture while not forgetting its place."

The house aligns almost entirely on one level at an elevation of 6,500 feet and contours with the mountain. It's defined by one long graceful line of a shed roof lifting up and out toward views of the Beartooth Mountains, with the cabin-like forms of the guestroom and owners' suite protruding in different directions from the main structure. The deck off the great room cantilevers dramatically out into open air. Utility spaces and a bedroom are anchored into the hillside end of the house, while the open kitchen, dining area, and living space are unified by concrete floors and an open three-sided fireplace and embrace 180-degree views.

The client's longtime interior designer, Alice Cramer, visited Montana for the first time to help realize clean, livable interiors in a subdued palette enlivened by pops of color. "It was an amazing opportunity," says the Atlanta-based designer. "My goal was that the end result for the interiors was as unique as the property and quite different from their other homes. Having worked with these clients on other projects, we can finish each other's sentences and with that comfort level comes trust. Trust is mandatory when working on projects that are in a different location from your primary home. Our approach was to complement the modern form and architecture and to create spaces that felt modern, but warm and inviting."

A mountainside home that seems a perfect fit for its place may have a sense of inevitability about it now, but was a long time in the making.

Inside, the rooms are grounded with contemporary furniture but filled out with well-chosen vintage pieces. The designer layered in texture and color through fabrics, rugs, and artwork to create a sense of warmth and comfort. Outside, multiple exterior spaces offer varied views and shelter depending on which way the wind is blowing, while intrusions into the landscape are minimal. The primary bedroom's sandstone terrace, for instance, is just large enough for two chaise longues, while an outdoor room with a stone fireplace and reclaimed wood ceiling nestles into the hillside where it's hidden from view and protected from the elements. The landscaping palette is designed to naturally blend into the native sagebrush and prairie grasses.

"We talk a lot about being indigenous to a region," says Tollefson. "The architecture and materiality of this home are local, and while there are aspects that might look elegant, such as the double cantilevered roof and deck, we never forget craftsmanship. This house is grounded in the ruggedness of the materials: the strength of the steel and stone and the texture of the wood. These ingredients are enough."

The homeowners of this mountain modern aerie near Red Lodge, Montana, traveled the greater Yellowstone area searching for the perfect property. The resulting home—designed by Pearson Design Group and built by OSM Construction—appears to emerge from the landscape, celebrating its place in steel, glass, regional stone, natural weathered wood, and other materials that speak to the surroundings.

Interior designer Alice Cramer paired the custom dining table with West Elm chairs and OCHRE lighting under a sheltering wood ceiling that holds the space against the immense open views. The kitchen marries book-matched marble and a custom light fixture with rustic materials.

OPPOSITE: In the primary bedroom, a graphic Patterson Flynn Martin rug grounds the room. The bench is from Robert James. A small patio, minimally furnished with Restoration Hardware chaises, gently edges into the landscape. Landscape architect Charlie Kees of Field Studio employed a minimal planting plan that defers to its alpine meadow environment.

LEFT: In the serene powder room, a pendant light from PALECEK illuminates the concrete counter with integrated sink.

The outdoor dining area, tucked between the house and a forested hillside, was conceived on a windy day when the importance of shelter from the elements was obvious. Furniture from Home Infatuation.

FRAMING THE LANDSCAPE

FRAMING
THE LANDSCAPE

No new experiences have a greater formative influence in the life of a child than summer camp. The weeks spent in nature foster self-reliance and create lasting memories, whether hiking, singing around the campfire, learning to tie knots, or problem-solving with a recalcitrant horse, a capsized canoe, or a leaking tent in a thunderstorm. But that feeling of living close to nature can be hard to replicate in adult life. Far too often, the yearning remains but goes unfulfilled. It's no wonder, then, that for a South Carolinian who grew up spending each summer in Minnesota's North Woods, a new life in Montana has renewed that unbridled joy in nature she experienced as a kid. As a bonus, she now gets to share that joy with her husband and grown children.

Although the couple owned property in the Allegheny Mountains, they dreamt of a home in the Rockies. With no ties to a particular community, they searched in Colorado, New Mexico, Idaho, and California before exploring Montana. In Bozeman, it all clicked. They looked at twenty properties, meeting Van Bryan of Studio Architects, builders Jamie Bottcher and Ryan Mann of Schlauch Bottcher Construction, and Abby Hetherington of Abby Hetherington Interiors in the process. The property they settled on is secluded, a 400-acre parcel west of town tucked up against Forest Service land at the north end of the Bridger Mountains. With uninterrupted views to the south and west, it's the perfect vantage point for watching thunderstorms advance up the valley. On clear nights, they can see the lights of Bozeman in the distance. There, just like at summer camp, immersion in nature is all-encompassing.

The first phase of the project involved building a mile-long access road and digging a pond to attract wildlife.

When it came to the design of the house, the husband leaned modern, the wife more contemporary rustic; the result is classic in form with modern interventions. The two-level house is arranged linearly along the hillside in distinct volumes that break up the massing. The main part of the house takes a simple gabled shape punctuated by a steel-clad chimney that dramatically thrusts through the roof and protrudes through a wall of windows on the view side. Inside, that same chimney, with its concrete hearth, injects decidedly modern energy into a home that marries rustic with contemporary. The rustic feel comes from the home's extensive use of reclaimed barnwood, which extends seamlessly from the outside in. The contemporary is manifested in a glass-box-like entry, unexpected furniture shapes and placement (like the large custom curved sofa facing the windows), and bold hues like hot pink and chartreuse. Large, color-infused paintings by Brian Rutenberg are set against plaster walls.

The couple are both artistic. The wife paints, sews, and makes pottery and jewelry, while the husband builds and paints model cars. Each has a studio or hobbyist workplace on-site in separate barn-like structures that host additional functions—one has a lap pool and full gym, and one has a party space.

The design process benefited from the marriage of creative minds, says architect Van Bryan. "We spent a great deal of time having very deliberate dialogues with the clients about how each space was going to look, how it would be taken care of, and how it would function. It made for a really engaging process; we had to get into the weeds early on so that we'd create design solutions that could handle [their lifestyle]. They were exceptional clients to work with, not only engaged but articulate. They left their fingerprints throughout the house—not that you would know that because our collaboration worked so well."

The owners were equally involved in the interior design. While Abby Hetherington is known for bold, original interior, even she and senior designer Chelsea Reetz were challenged to think differently. The powder room features chartreuse green; in the dining room, the client pushed for a vibrant fuchsia. One barn features red lacquered cabinets and, in the bathroom, red wallpaper. "The client wanted that punch," Hetherington says. "And it was really fun because she took it somewhere we never would have thought it could go."

Beyond the punchy hues and patterns, it was about considering every detail for a modern, welcoming environment, adds the designer. "Everything is built in, thoughtful, simple; every corner was thought out. We made sure everything was structured but that all the textures were soft and comfortable and that, tonality-wise, everything worked together." As a result and even with some generous volumes, the home is welcoming and cozy enough that the couple already lives there most of the year.

For the wife, who grew up hiking and camping in the woods, it's been like coming home. "I felt I'd been waiting for this move all my life," she says. "Lowcountry life was lovely and we made some very good friends there. Here in Montana, though, I feel that I'm living the life I was made for, in the place I was meant to be."

"My taste for this home was what we call 'contemporary rustic,'" says the homeowner of a series of structures designed by Van Bryan of Studio Architects and built by Schlauch Bottcher Construction on four hundred acres outside of Bozeman, Montana. Throughout the house, vibrant art by painter Brian Rutenberg sets the tone, especially in the dining room where the rug and chairs take their color cues from the painting. The fuchsia chairs are from Egg & Dart with fabric from Osborne & Little. The OVUUD chandelier adds an organic feel to the rectilinear space.

"For the kitchen and butler's pantry," says designer Abby Hetherington of Hetherington Interiors, "we wanted the island to be the focal point. We used Black Diamond leathered slabs for the island and backsplash. The idea was for the kitchen to be just as pretty even when nothing was out." The pendants are from Allied Maker; the stools are Room & Board with a Holly Hunt fabric. They used a matte finish in the kitchen, but in the darker pantry chose lacquered cabinets to reflect the light.

The client wanted the primary bedroom to feel soft and organic. Neutral shades reign in the Roman shade with Harlequin fabric, the custom bed by Russ Fry, and custom swivel chair by Barahona. Kelly Wearstler sconces give a knowing nod to Native American tepees.

OVERLEAF, LEFT: A cozy, quiet space to watch a movie, take a phone call, or enjoy a libation utilizes glass panels to create privacy without separation.

OVERLEAF, RIGHT: A local vendor, Old Main, created the custom mirrors hanging above the DeMuro Das cabinets. The movement in the Hubbardton Forge Wave chandelier speaks to the pattern in the rug.

A sense of transparency is announced from the moment of entry, with glass-and-steel doors that swing wide open and views that look straight through the house to distant mountains. The driftwood artworks on either side of the door serve as reminders of the home's place in the landscape.

MONTANA MINIMALIST

MONTANA MINIMALIST

The pandemic years have forever changed the way we think about work. For a couple who lived all over the world before finding themselves empty-nesting in Michigan, their move to Montana makes the most of the work-from-home movement. In the process, their daily "commute" has morphed—from one defined by traffic lights to one that celebrates the play of light.

In this modern cabin designed by architect Doug Minarik for a hillside site outside Bozeman, light—how it moves, how it changes over the course of the day, how it plays on the home's multitoned wood walls and ceilings—is a central theme. An accompanying theme is sense of place.

"This project was all about this long, linear experience and breaking up each little snippet of the view," the architect explains. "Typically, you come into a house, and it's like, 'There's your view.' But we had this concept of the morning commute and the evening commute, where, as you move across this line of topography, you get a different snippet of the mountains depending on what you're doing. The morning light coming in this hallway is really pretty, and it's activated differently as you move through different spaces in the house."

The building sits at an elevation of 5,000 feet on a knoll surrounded by trees facing north to open high-altitude hillsides on the opposite side of the canyon. It is revealed by degrees, barely visible from the winding road below; as you ascend the drive, only one end can be glimpsed through a screen of aspens. The house presents as a simple shed-roof structure that extends along the contour line of the hillside, disappearing into and creating a crisp contrast to its sylvan setting. Its fire-blackened shou sugi ban exterior is lightened by

wood soffits under the metal roof and a board-formed concrete foundation.

Minarik worked to align all the functions of the home under one continuous roofline while allowing for split levels on either end of the house. On one end, the garage tucks below, while inside there's a half-level step up to the primary bedroom suite; on the other end, an upstairs lounge floats above a two-bedroom guest wing. The entry is positioned toward the middle of the structure where a long, narrow deck captures warmth and sunlight. Alternating fir wood and glass panels lend a musicality to the exterior design. Inside, they admit a serene quality of light and cast shadows that change over the course of the day, and over the course of the season.

The structure is simple, with the primary bedroom and guest wing anchoring the ends, and the long hallway tying them together. The center of the home is occupied by the main poplar-lined living space, with its window wall looking out to glorious mountain views. A protected outdoor room, adjacent to the living room and carved out of the exterior, is exposed to the elements on just one side. With an ultra-efficient wood stove, the space allows for year-round outdoor living.

A minimalist structure calls for minimalist interiors. Minarik worked with Portland-based tile manufacturer Clayhaus on most of the tile; the clients selected honed granite for the kitchen countertops. In the loft, they chose a wallpaper that was subdued but still popped. "Most of the residential projects we work on are pretty stripped back, so there isn't a lot of room for extra layers of decisions," says the architect. "As a result, the fixed elements are integral to the overall design. The clients put a lot of trust in our selections and in creating

Light—how it moves, how it changes over the course of the day, how it plays on the home's multitoned wood walls and ceilings—is central in this modern cabin.

a comprehensive design, and the wife has a wonderfully eclectic sense of style, which is evident through their art collection. She pushed us to go beyond our architecturally tidy ways."

A highly personal house, many of its details respond to the couple's unique set of wishes. Clean lines were prioritized: the bar, TV, pantry, and kitchen equipment disappear behind wood doors. The owners didn't want to see hardware as they passed through the house, so the contractor and architect designed retracting door handles. The wife dreamt of a tub with a view, the husband had a vision for a cigar lounge, and they both wanted direct access to the outdoors from their bedroom. The clients wanted to minimize wasted space but still dwell in a house that could easily contract and expand as needed. (While modest in scale and impact, the owners can live large with guests overflowing into a barn apartment—an existing structure that Minarik totally opened up and reconfigured—and an Airstream

trailer.) Most importantly, they were adamant that the building slot unobtrusively into its site, minimize its impact, and eschew any pretense of grandeur.

This is a house for all seasons. In the summertime, bears wander through the property, filling up on blackberries, which are plentiful because the homeowners have left so much of the land undisturbed. Springtime coats the hills in bright green and wildlife with their young are abundant. In the fall, the aspens turn a vibrant yellow; when the elk bugle, the owners run upstairs to see them through a scope looking out on the high open meadows across the valley. Winter brings heavy snowfall, sometimes stranding them at home for days at a time. With all three of their daughters living in Montana, Thanksgiving is a particularly meaningful time to celebrate the house. They move furniture out of the way in the great room, crank up the wood stove, and run two long tables end to end to accommodate everyone. Then they give thanks for their Montana life.

A Montana home designed by architect Doug Minarik and built by Archer Construction achieves an extraordinary grace in its clarity of expression and movement of light. Poplar wood cladding on the walls and ceiling and Douglas fir flooring create a quiet beauty within which the Deer Damask wallpaper from Barneby Gates pops. A Hans Wegner shell chair adds sculptural grace.

RIGHT: The seemingly simple shed-roofed structure is rendered in two main volumes: one for the primary bedroom and bath and one for the gathering rooms, with guest rooms on the far end tucked under an outdoor lounge. Nestled into the hillside and foliage above a winding valley road, the home's generous views look across to open meadows on high foothills. The shou sugi ban siding was sourced from Nakamoto Forestry; the contrasting soffits and wall cladding are fir.

OVERLEAF: The owners of this home have an aversion to drywall, so they and the architect decided early on that poplar would be used throughout 90 percent of the home's interiors. To counter the tendency of poplar to take on a green hue, each board was dipped in an acid wash to neutralize and set the tone of the wood.

LEFT: This is a home in which everything has its place and can be put away, even the kitchen. The poplar doors fold open for use and, when shut, merge seamlessly with the walls. The Haiku ceiling fan is from Big Ass Fans, the dining table from Architect's Wife in Bozeman.

OVERLEAF, LEFT: Contemporary rustic barn doors hung on Krownlab Barn Door Hardware slide out of the way when open.

OVERLEAF, RIGHT: The primary bedroom has colorful artwork, floor-to-ceiling windows, and an indoor/outdoor feel.

PAGE 104: The guest rooms share a lounge area partially carved out from under the stairs.

PAGE 105: In the primary bath, Avallon Navy tiles from the Cement Tile Shop add color and movement; the Pili Pendant by Arturo Alverez offers whimsy and a sense of lightness. The tub is from Kingston Brass. The narrow window was a deliberate choice, explains the architect. "Window openings were carefully sized so that as you move throughout the house, your view to the north is constantly being reset and rescaled. In the main bathroom, we used a tall, narrow sliver of glass to celebrate the layers, from field to mountain to sky."

INDUSTRIAL
FRAMEWORK

INDUSTRIAL
FRAMEWORK

As a building material, board-formed concrete injects a certain level of contradiction into a project. It is man-made yet imprinted with a touch of the natural. It has an industrial feel yet carries with it a warmth through tone and texture. Formed with wood boards that are then stripped away, it takes advantage of the plasticity, strength, and durability of concrete while celebrating the natural imperfections—and the natural beauty—of wood.

The material seems tailor-made for modernists seeking a new form of expression in the Mountain West, yet it wasn't that long ago that residential architects were only tentatively suggesting it to their clients. Larry Pearson of Pearson Design Group had long been interested in the potential for rustic modern environments created with board-formed concrete, glass, steel, and reclaimed wood. On a sixty-acre site outside Jackson, Wyoming, he found the perfect setting and ideal clients with whom to collaborate in bringing this vision to life.

The property's existing house was well positioned on a promontory raised up from the valley floor. From that vantage point, it enjoyed a strong sense of privacy amidst mature trees, as well as stunning views of the Snake River and Teton Mountains. After extensive planning to renovate the house, though, it became apparent that it made more sense to start over. But when Pearson and project architect Josh Barr suggested board-formed concrete and steel as primary building materials, the owners weren't so sure.

Originally, says the wife, "I kept thinking farmhouse modern, but when I asked Larry to draw his vision, he was leaning more modern. The whole spine and front of the house were going to be board-formed concrete. It was a little out of my comfort zone, but my husband was all for it. I said, 'Guys, I'm from Texas. If we do this, we have to have a lot of warm materials, like reclaimed white oak floors, to soften it. We're going to have to warm this up. We can't build a concrete box.' And they said, 'Absolutely, let's do this!'"

The home's exterior is defined by expanses of board-formed concrete punctuated with large panes of glass that reflect the mountains and trees, barnwood applied both horizontally and vertically, stonework, and beams of steel and reclaimed wood. The structure is laid out on two perpendicular axes defined by spines of board-formed concrete, which visibly extrude at either end of the east-west axis. From the entry on the south side to the great room and the covered patio on the north, the roof slopes upward to embrace the views. There, paired chimneys of stone and steel thrust dramatically upward, piercing the wood-clad roof and anchoring the home to its site.

The architects and their contractor colleagues at OSM Construction orchestrated this symphony of materiality with intervals of opacity and transparency, emphasized by glass-cornered bedrooms and a foyer with floor-to-ceiling glass walls on opposite sides. "At the time," recalls Larry Pearson, "we were experimenting with a number of ideas that were very novel. The two perpendicular spines of board-formed concrete anchored the house to the site and [took advantage of the] panoramic views, and the transparency of the glass opened up to the site. So there's a tension in these spaces with the protective solidity of the concrete walls, and the big glass faces with views to the Tetons and the

As an early iteration of a rustic modern aesthetic, the house succeeds on many levels and exemplifies the warmth and soulfulness of seemingly industrial materiality.

valley floor. That was the principle of the house in its conception."

The main program resides on the entry level. The kitchen, dining area, great room, and patio occupy the heart of the building; the primary and secondary suites punctuate the ends, where they benefit from privacy and views. With the land sloping gently away below the main outdoor living area, the lower level—comprised of a media room, two bedroom suites, and a gathering room—extends outside to a patio with fireplace and spa. This affords the deck above the perfect vantage point to appreciate the reflection of the Tetons in the pond below.

The interiors were designed by Michon Anne Combs of MC Design. "My first goal," says the designer, "was to try to keep them as quiet as possible because I wanted the focus to be on the outdoors. And the house itself is so beautiful, the materials and the shell are so gorgeous, I didn't want to fight it too much. Over the years we've added more [details] to make it a little bit warmer and more layered. But the approach at first was to keep everything super quiet to allow the architecture to take the lead."

Ceilings of white oak with a warm red patina play against board-formed concrete walls and reclaimed barnwood. The doors of chunky, hand-adzed reclaimed wood comprise a neutral but textured backdrop for comfortable furnishings in earth tones and understated colors. The kitchen is set up for ease of entertaining with custom cabinetry and double islands—one concrete topped, one marble with waterfall sides. A custom hood of black steel adds a dramatic moment. The owner combined suede dining chairs with a metal-topped table, designed a sumptuous sofa in mauve, and spent six months sourcing key lighting pieces from European workshops.

As an early iteration of a rustic modern aesthetic, the house succeeds on many levels and exemplifies the warmth and soulfulness of seemingly industrial materiality. "The idea of contrast between the organic and inorganic is part of the principle at work here," says Pearson. "I like that in a contemporary design—that tension that's created between an industrial product like a steel table and concrete, which can be industrial, and tensioning that against a raw wood wall. You're mixing these assemblies in such a way that they accent each other; the concrete frame and the boards almost become the artwork that exists within the concrete frame. It's the organic and inorganic tension that defines this house."

A house on sixty sublime acres near Wilson, Wyoming, is built of reclaimed boards, reclaimed white oak, natural patinaed steel, limestone veneer, and board-formed concrete. It maintains a remarkably simple and consistent palette throughout, lending it an ethereal air—unusual in a home that emphasizes industrial materials. Pearson Design Group's Larry Pearson and Josh Barr proposed board-formed concrete and steel as the primary building materials; OSM Construction brought it to fruition.

The quiet dining nook in the kitchen demonstrates the beauty and integrity of the materials when combined with muted, monochromatic tones and carefully placed artwork.

LEFT: Designer Michon Anne Combs of MC Design crafted the interiors in a home where structure plays a visible role, such as over the stairwell and circulation areas. A large open-sided fireplace separates the dining room from the gathering room while injecting a feeling of warmth to the entire open living area, amplified by the rose-colored sofa. A Lindsey Adelman light fixture extends the feeling of lightness within seemingly heavy materials. The living room lighting is by Apparatus Studio; the furnishings from Baxter, Poltrona Frau, and Maxalto, with select finds from Round Top market in Texas.

OVERLEAF, LEFT: In the office, art by Robert Mars works well with a Kelley Wearstler chair and Maxalto desk.

OVERLEAF, RIGHT: Carefully ordered built-in bookshelves against an exposed reclaimed wood wall frame a collection of books and objects. Reclaimed white oak ceilings and reclaimed French white oak floors carry through the entire structure.

The primary bedroom is all about the double-sided fireplace and highlighting the home's placement on a promontory, which allows the utmost in privacy as well as enjoyment of big views of the Tetons, Snake River, and valley. The steel-lined wood storage compartment doubles as contemporary artwork.

The neutral palette of the home extends to the bathrooms. The primary bathroom has a tub and floating vanity by **NEUTRA** with fixtures from **Pinch** and **VOLA**. In the powder room, the Non Random Light from **Moooi** illuminates the Kreoo marble sink bowl. An iron artwork by Matt Devine pops against the board-formed concrete backdrop.

SOLACE IN
THE TETONS

SOLACE IN
THE TETONS

The couple had been searching for the perfect place to transition to their new life as empty-nesters when they came upon a "for sale" sign marking a five-acre parcel perched on the westernmost edge of a steep ridge in Jackson Hole. The property had a top-of-the-world feeling, both elevated above and immersed in the grandeur of the Teton Mountains. Stunning panoramic vistas stretched from Powder Peak to Grand Teton while the Snake River wended its way through the valley, farmlands, and open pastures below. The sense of space and light and the majesty of the mountains was captivating; the feeling of being one with the environment—from sunrises and sunsets to summer thunderstorms and winter whiteouts—was absolutely exhilarating. "When you find a piece of land like that, with those views, it's a once-in-a-lifetime opportunity," says the homeowner. "We'd found that perfect fit."

Rendezvous Design's principal designer, Patricia Kennedy, had lived in New York and studied in Paris. She spent eight years in Asia focusing on wellness design, including feng shui and wabi-sabi and pursued sustainable, accessible, and biophilic (inspired by nature) design at the New York School of Interior Design. As a native Texan living on the East Coast who was now experiencing the overwhelming impact of the site, she found a vision taking shape. She imagined a mountain modern home—perched 500 feet above the valley floor and cradled in the rugged embrace of the Tetons—that would marry the sophistication of contemporary architecture with the serenity of nature.

Kennedy collaborated with Northworks Architects on the conceptualization of the structure and with Teton Heritage Builders on the construction. For this deeply personal project she was inspired by Mies van der Rohe's Farnsworth House, circa 1950, acclaimed for its clarity of expression and immersion into the surrounding environment. "It was my inspiration, the perfect 'parti' on which to base the home. I loved the simplicity, panoramic glazing, and connection to nature."

Farnsworth House's influence on this house is evident in its modern form, a glazed pavilion with flanking decks, the cantilevered banquette punctuating the façade, and its adherence to golden mean proportions, a mathematically harmonious ratio that dates back to ancient Greece. The two-level, 4,800-square-foot residence harmonizes with the hillscape by using such sustainable materials as reclaimed barnwood, metal, and Accoya wood, which ground the structure in its wild setting. At the entry-level, the home encompasses living spaces, the primary suite, and outdoor entertaining areas. Three additional bedrooms, a game room, and a workout room, as well as a spa and sauna, are built into the hillside below.

As one steps across the threshold, the home reveals its true nature in a proprioceptive, multisensory experience designed to prioritize wellness-inducing principles: honoring sightlines, introducing natural elements, and engaging the trio of mind-body-senses. To engage the mind, the designer considers "gaze sequencing," or how one experiences the views, as well as spatial navigation and energy flow. This enhances one's journey through the home by highlighting key design features and creating a connection to nature. Engaging the body means planning for the future through accessibility design, including single-level living, easy-to-access appliances and storage, nonslip

Peace of Jackson is a living, breathing testament to the transformative power of mindful design.

flooring, smart lighting and shading, and a design that allows for an elevator shaft in the future. To engage the senses, Kennedy incorporates textured elements, personalized scent, and nature-streaming soundscapes to transform the day-to-day living experience. Honoring these principles, she explains, creates a canvas for calm and inspires relaxation, rejuvenation, and a sense of well-being.

For the interiors, Kennedy followed neurosensorial design principles—her trademarked methodology combining neuroaesthetics with sensorial design—to create spaces that resonate on multiple levels. These play out in details like biophilic accents of textured walnut flooring, pebbled tiles, forested wallpapers, mineral furnishings, organic textiles, fire and water elements, and, of course, the views. A cedar-lined Finnish sauna, eucalyptus-infused steam shower, color therapy soaking tub, and outdoor hot tub further promote wellness. Commissioned contemporary artworks from artists such as Duke Beardsley, Miles Glynn, and Jo Sherwood add pops of color and unique personality to the spaces.

The heart of the home is the great room, where panoramic glazing creates a natural observatory for migrating wildlife, the changing seasons, and spectacular views of the Teton Range. There, the seating area is anchored by a large sofa and grounded by a black leathered granite hearth and wood-burning fireplace with wood storage. Organic sun-bleached wood slices in the coffee table offer a biophilic moment. Heated floors of wire-brushed walnut add comfort during the winter months, while custom Lutron-controlled LEDs create

light scenes for various modes, from "wake up" to "party." The living space opens out to an expansive outdoor deck with comfortable seating, a firepit, infrared heaters, and an outdoor kitchen and dining area.

The home balances beauty and elegance in furnishings with a sense of playfulness. The great room and kitchen are delineated by a shuffleboard, a much-used game table that acts as a dynamic social hub then effortlessly converts to a dining table for twelve. A swing positioned in the corner of the great room perfectly frames the mountain vignette for new arrivals; when someone climbs in, they see a floor insert depicting prominent mountains in the landscape.

When the house was included in the Jackson Hole Showcase of Homes, Kennedy found that visitors felt at ease immediately upon entering. And they lingered, hanging out on the deck, relaxing on the sofas, and swaying in the swing. They were also full of questions about biophilic design. That immersion in nature is, after all, why people are drawn to places like Jackson; its architecture and interiors, Kennedy notes, should reflect that. "By incorporating biophilia, you make the home feel really grounded and connected," she says. "I think the purpose of living here is to honor sense of place with a home that harmonizes with its natural setting. Peace of Jackson is a living, breathing testament to the transformative power of mindful design. It invites its inhabitants to pause, breathe, and reconnect with the primal beauty of nature, offering a profound sense of peace and well-being. Here, wellness is not just a feature but the very essence of living."

Perched 500 feet above the valley floor and clad in sustainable reclaimed barnwood and FSC-certified Accoya, a home by Rendezvous Design blends into the native sagebrush hillscape. The great room combines a black leathered granite hearth, organic textiles, goat fur poufs, and a circle swing. The deck extends outdoor living with an Outer sofa and Coyote grill and smoker.

In the living space, the dining table converts to a shuffleboard. The contemporary cowboy painting is by Duke Beardsley; the custom neon artwork is by Miles Glynn.

WRANGLING THE FAMILY

WRANGLING
THE FAMILY

Newcomers to the West often want to build up high and exposed, the better to dramatize the views. Ranchers and farmers, however, have historically built down low, choosing a sheltered spot amongst the trees for protection from the elements. Practicality ruled: ease of access, proximity to water, and the ability to check on the livestock were all deciding factors. The Seattle-based owners of a Montana ranch considering a summer retreat looked no further than a level area in a cottonwood grove on the edge of cattle pasture. The spot was an easy walk to the fishing waters of Big Timber Creek, hummed with wildlife, and sported exhilarating views north to the peaks of the Crazy Mountains—the perfect location for a rustic modern compound.

Years before, explains Paul Bertelli of JLF Architects, the client had envisioned a significantly more ambitious project, with designs for a lodge, barn, and caretaker's house. "As we went through the process, though, our client realized she just wasn't sure if it was the right thing. We took a pause, we talked more about the program, and she said it was really meant to be more like camp for them. That turned into 'Let's do interesting small spaces. We're good at improvising and putting people where they need to be, whether on a couch or sleeping bag, and it will feel more like a summer camp.' It has so much charm they've found they use it more. Now they've asked us to add to it, but they want to keep it at the same scale because the more gently we build on the landscape, the more it's about place."

The initial concept indicated prefab buildings, but after significant research they came to the conclusion that, done right, they could build custom for less. Big-D Signature/Dovetail Construction was brought in to build the primary structure—a gathering space with kitchen, living room, and screened porch—and two small-scaled sleeping cabins, identical in layout and limited in scope to a bedroom, bathroom, and deck. "The concept called for narrow footprints in structures without complex roof pitches," Bertelli says. "We would build using simple, honest materials like galvanized steel components. Nothing would be custom bent or custom made, but we could add details. We'd use materials that will weather and have a sense of timelessness about them. We created flexible multiuse spaces and purposely made the bedrooms just small enough to put a bed in so that everyone would gather in the main cabin."

The main cabin, of reclaimed-wood siding with a standing-seam metal roof, is gabled on either end. Its middle section is defined by a shed roof that lifts up to take in views of the Crazy Mountains to the north. There, a large deck with tall glass doors runs the length of the structure, dramatically expanding the living space, with a steel pergola offering a sense of shelter. On the eastern end, a comfortable screened porch offers intimate views into the cottonwoods, while on the south side, a small deck with four tall doors opening onto it guides guests to the entry. The sleeping cabins, constructed of the same materials, also have shed roofs oriented toward the primary views, along with small decks partially protected by their overhanging roofs.

Tim Rote of Dovetail Construction oversaw the build, as well as a refresh of two existing cabins, a storage shed, and a barn. He found the project an exercise in thoughtful simplicity. "All the exposed structural elements are structural steel with a finish to mimic galvanization; those are connected to galvanized steel studs commonly

By designing a compound of human-scaled homes that defers to the landscape and sits lightly on the land, the owners find themselves immersed in nature rather than merely observing it.

used in commercial framing applications," he says. "The mix of the commercial galvanized steel elements with reclaimed wood plays off two very different but beautiful materials. It's not that often that you see architecture pushing that envelope. It brings a whole other meaning of timelessness to it. I don't think you'll ever look at this place and be able to say when this was built."

For interiors, WRJ Design embraced the challenge of designing and sourcing rugged, timeless furnishings that would stand up to heavy use. "On a ranch, you don't want to worry about putting your feet on a coffee table or getting a sofa dirty," says designer Rush Jenkins. "We try to approach these projects as comfortable but not precious. Since there's a lot of dirt, dust, and traffic on a ranch, you have to make sure the materials won't be destroyed. If someone has a ranch and wants it to be a reminder of what the Old West was and how a ranching family lives, it's not about the furnishings or luxury. It's about function, comfort, and conversation. It's about

connecting with those around you. And after the hard work and hard play that comes with the lifestyle, at the end of the day, you want to put your head on a nice pillow with the windows open and the fresh air coming through your bedroom and be able to hear the crickets and wilderness."

By designing a compound of human-scaled homes that defers to the landscape and sits lightly on the land, the owners find themselves immersed in nature rather than merely observing it. Nestled among the cottonwoods on the edge of cattle pasture, they can watch the birds in the grasses and listen to the wind in the trees. In winter, when the trees are bare, they can see sunlight glinting off the waters of the creek. At night, when they leave the gathering space to head back to their beds, they step into the grass underneath a brilliant night sky—and, for at least a moment, are taken back to that feeling of awe and wonder at their place in the world.

Nestled into a grove of cottonwoods near Big Timber Creek in Montana, a modern rustic compound on a cattle ranch was designed by JLF Architects and built by Big-D Signature/Dovetail Construction. The goal was "interesting small spaces," with sleeping cabins separated from the main gathering spot. Every room throughout the compound is focused on the outdoors, and each structure is built from simple, honest materials. WRJ Design did the interiors for easy indoor/outdoor living, adding just enough texture to create a sense of refuge.

PRECEDING OVERLEAF: The living area opens onto a deck with a pergola of galvanized steel and a screened porch of reclaimed wood.

LEFT: The kitchen is a study in simplicity, with the focus on easy provisioning for members of an extended family who are coming in and going out all day as they head off on adventures in nature. The countertops are Caesarstone quartz. The wall paneling and cabinets are oak plywood with oak batten strips.

OVERLEAF, LEFT: A guest cabin amplifies the back-at-camp vibes with four bunks for family togetherness. The lighting pendant adds a contemporary element.

OVERLEAF, RIGHT: Exposed galvanized structural metal studs give a pleasing rhythm to the architecture of the deck.

This family compound is all about the outdoors. Simple, human-scaled structures defer to the landscape.

ESCAPE TO THE LAKE

ESCAPE TO THE LAKE

When a time-tested creative team reunites with a favorite client on a project doubly blessed with a phenomenal site and fun-centric program, the results can be sublime. This was true for this group's project at the Yellowstone Club. A waterfront property on Hebgen Lake, located just outside West Yellowstone, Montana, offered the perfect opportunity to continue the creative camaraderie.

The owners were attracted to Hebgen Lake for its scenic beauty and off-the-beaten-path vibe. Fed by the Madison River and created by Hebgen Dam in 1914, the 15-mile-long lake is mostly surrounded by public land. The few private lots that do exist come up for sale infrequently, engendering a laid-back, generational feel in a place where it's all about immersing in nature.

The couple approached the property with intention. An existing cabin came with rodents and sagging beams, but they lived with it through two seasons to get to know the land and weather patterns before entering the design stage with their reunited team: architect Greg Matthews of Greg Matthews Studio; interior designers Rain Houser and Skye Anderson of Urbaine Atelier; and builder Chris Lohss of Lohss Construction.

The site is blessed with mature vegetation, including 100-foot-tall spruce trees and an enormous willow next to the lake. "The clients loved all the mature trees and didn't want to compromise them," explains the architect. "And it was a no-brainer; you had this monumental specimen willow tree and the cottonwoods and aspens as the elements creating the armature to frame views of the lake."

"A good lake house always has a connection to the water and to the lawn activities," Matthews continues.

"From the beginning, it was obvious that the primary living space would be in the zone to frame the views and the experience of the lake. That was intuitive. But the goal of any one of our projects is for it to feel like it's been there for decades. If we can do that right, it's a job well done. We wove the footprint in and out of the trees to reinforce that sense of belonging from the very first day. That was critical to the success of this project, and it meant that the integration of the house into the landscape was almost immediate."

Matthews created a wending approach from the road leading to the home, which is perched at water's edge for total immersion in the lake experience. The design employs a practical simplicity without losing its wow factor. The four-bedroom, 2,400-square-foot home doubles in usable space with adjacent outdoor living areas and maintains a strong connection to the lake; its lower deck cantilevers out over the water while its interior experience is all about that open expanse of water, sky, and mountains. The exterior is expressed in glass, steel, and wood, with visible structural steel as a key component of the design. Two roofs provide dramatic tension, with one pitching up toward the entry to create a sense of welcome and the other facing south, lifting up toward the lake and expansive views of the Madison mountain range. "The two roof planes are interwoven and stitched together," he says. "I wanted to keep it simple but also let the geometry of the roof welcome you into the house then open up toward what this property is all about, which is the water and the mountains. They're stitched together to keep it simple, but they reinforce the arrival and the experience of the place."

When the Fourth of July rolls around and all three children, their partners, and grandchildren take up residence, the house fulfills its highest and best use.

Interiors dominated by glass and polished concrete floors are warmed by white fir ceilings that carry the eye outside. The rooms are grounded in neutrals with dark green and terra-cotta accents and softened with textural chandeliers and furnishings with natural fibers. "Studio green appears in the kitchen, on the lounge chairs, and in a large bowl on the living room table," says Houser. "Terra-cotta is mixed throughout, on the backsplash in the kitchen and in the pendants over the island. Blending warm natural tones with the cool of the bleached wood coffee table and the leather chandelier with gray tones is really nice and suits the space."

Unusual touches include an outdoor dining counter with four stools facing the lake; a wraparound multilevel deck whose lowest level functions as a swim platform and dock; a steel fireplace set within the great room's glass wall; and a backsplash of handmade Moroccan tiles in the kitchen. One bedroom suite is only accessible from outside, enhancing the sense of romance and privacy for guests. In the entry, a wildlife painting by Amy Ringholz, commissioned specifically for the project, firmly grounds the home in its place on the edge of the Yellow-stone wilderness.

When the Fourth of July rolls around and all three children, their partners, and grandchildren take up residence, the house fulfills its highest and best use: the doors are wide open, with wet kids running through the house, and people grilling on the deck, reading in the lounge chairs, pulling up to the deck on jet skis, or cannonballing into the water. After all, says Houser, "This house is all about the lake."

Perched on the edge of Hebgen Lake in southwest Montana, the glass-and-steel retreat designed by Greg Matthews Studio and built by Lohss Construction doubles in size with the outdoor living space. Rain Houser and Skye Anderson of Urbaine Atelier created moments of coziness with color and texture. A large-scale linen fiber chandelier and Verellen dining table anchor the dining area, while the colorful papier-mâché fish by artist Adair Peck add a touch of whimsy.

RIGHT: Artwork commissioned from Amy Ringholz greets guests in the entry. The one-of-a-kind stools—made from reclaimed springs and upholstered with vintage rugs—speak to the vintage rug on the floor, which was hand selected by Urbaine Atelier during a trip to Morocco. The rope sconces are from Luke Lamp Company.

OVERLEAF, LEFT: A light-filled open kitchen features barstools from McGuire and custom white oak cabinetry painted a soft green. The cylindrical hood is a minimal presence in front of the window.

OVERLEAF, RIGHT: In the living room, a cascading leather chandelier above a vintage rug adds a touch of Boho glamour. The faux bois side table is vintage; the colorful bowl is Moroccan. The embroidered feather pillows are from Coral & Tusk.

ABOVE: A clean aesthetic prevails in the bathrooms of a house that's all about ease of living. Faucet from Crosswater; hand towel bar from SIN; custom cabinetry.

OPPOSITE: A cozy bedroom with a sliding door brings in colors from nature through hues of green and blue in a settee from Ligne Roset and artwork by Kene Sperry.

It's all about the lake at this family retreat: cantilevered decks are within jumping distance of the water. The outdoor furniture by Loll is made from recycled materials. The sense of integration of the house into the landscape makes all the difference on this project, says architect Greg Matthews. "We wove the footprint in and out of the trees to reinforce a sense of belonging from the very first day it was completed."

FRENCH BOHEMIA

FRENCH BOHEMIA

Fiona Louppe West was a French teenager on a family trip to Jackson Hole when she had an epiphany. "I remember sitting by the Snake River looking at the mountains and realizing I never wanted to leave." Since then, West has crafted a life that allows her to follow her Western-leaning heart.

One day on a road trip in her twenties, she woke up in Paradise Valley, Montana, awestruck by the scenery. Year after year she returned, eventually purchasing a home, and figuring out how to work remotely (even pre-pandemic) as president of Pierre Frey, the iconic French fabric brand. During the pandemic she enrolled her son in a Montana school and never left. Her calendar is punctuated by frequent trips to Paris, New York, and global design centers, but her life is of the West, complete with a log cabin and farm animals. "It's a privilege to be somewhere physically and mentally where you feel you're in the right place," she says. "People who know me professionally are astonished when I say where I live, but the people who've called me Laura Ingalls all my life say, 'You've always loved this stuff.'"

West had been splitting her time between Miami Beach and Paradise Valley when her landlord informed her that she was selling the house. Prices had skyrocketed, so she knew she had to act quickly. Then she saw an unappealing advertisement for a property that was located on a road named for the convicts who built it. It had languished on the market for two years but she immediately saw its potential. Despite its 1980s provenance, the log house had the feel of a homestead, tucked out of site of the rural road that winds along the river. Built with a sheltering berm on its backside, the home looks across a broad open meadow to a line of cottonwoods along the Yellowstone River. And in the distance—mountains.

"At first, I was taken aback," she admits. "The house wasn't very pretty, and it had a lot of red roofing. But the volumes were great, and the property had so much going for it: river frontage, amazing views, lots of acreage, and it was fifteen minutes from town. But I loved the big main space in the center; I loved the fact there was a cabin and lots of trees. When you spend time in Montana, you know those are important features. I thought if I tackled this in a smart way, little by little, I could transform this place."

Transforming a dark, outdated house into a France-meets-the-mountains-with-a-dash-of-Bohemia home is an ongoing process. West undertakes one significant project a year but is always fielding ideas, making improvements, and rearranging furniture and art. (To come: a wraparound porch with a new mudroom entry.) She tackled the living room first, tearing out the carpet and refinishing the floors but keeping the river-rock detail. She painted the ceiling white and redesigned the kitchen, removing upper cabinets, installing white beadboard, and adding a woodblock countertop and a large marble-topped island. She reconfigured bathrooms and applied her unique touch to every room in the house and guest cabin.

West's furnishings are a blend of antiques, family heirlooms, and significant objects mixed with art brought from France, where she was raised among artists. She also enjoys collecting work by Montana artists. Her use of Pierre Frey fabrics and rugs adds to the European country aesthetic while providing injections of color and energy into wood-dominated rooms. In her bedroom, she went for a moody feel with a panoramic wallpaper

> "I think a property always needs to be evolving with your life."

on one wall—the rich greens, blues, and beiges creating a feeling of calm. In the guest room, curtains made from hand-embroidered Pierre Frey fabric feature colorfully garmented African women. An exuberant floral drape camouflaging bathroom storage is paired with hand-cut Moroccan tiles. Her son's bedroom is cozy and colorful, with a Pierre Frey rug and lots of bookshelves. "I love eclecticism," West explains, "and using fabrics and wallpapers that I've collected over the years. I've dared to mix it all up, and it's fun and colorful. My philosophy is not to worry too much about whether things go together but trust that if I like it, it will come together."

West appreciates the thought that went into the orientation and structure of the house, nearby cabin, and garage/workshop. "Whatever the season, it's cozy and bright and that's one of the things I love about this place. I wanted to make it feel welcoming and sophisticated but relaxed—a place where people can just take their shoes off and sit on the floor, where kids can move around and make a mess. The house is full of life and I'm constantly changing and evolving it.

"In the U.S., there's an obsession with having a perfect place," she adds. "In Europe, you make do with what's there. We have a saying in France: "Make your own sauce." It means find your own flavor and figure out how you're going to adapt a space. Coming up with design solutions within the constraints of a space and budget is cool. A lot of people would have bulldozed the house, but I love what it's becoming. A property always needs to be evolving with your life, with the people who come into your life, and with your changing tastes and needs. That is the beauty of it. That, and coming to terms with the fact that it's imperfect."

As a young girl in Paris, Fiona West was always drawn to the American West she saw on television and in movies. As an adult she chose to move to Montana and works from there as president of the French fabric company Pierre Frey. In refreshing her 1980s log house, she says, "I wanted to work with the warm tones of the wood walls yet break the wood-cabin feel, integrating art and pops of color." The living room combines artwork from her friend Nina Johnson's art gallery in Miami with vintage cowboy hats, a lighting fixture from Apparatus, and a coffee table crafted from a vintage Indonesian bed. "The rug [from Pierre Frey, of course] makes this room!"

PRECEDING OVERLEAF:
West wanted the kitchen to have an open feel, she explains, in order "for the kitchen to not feel like a kitchen, but rather like an integral part of the living room." Timeless white beadboard with one continuous open shelf pairs well with wood countertops, floors, and walls, all bathed in light from the skylight. Artwork by family friend Pierre Tal-Coat hangs over a vintage marble-and-wood vanity from the early 1900s next to drapery embroidery from Pierre Frey. The plates and bowls are by Montana ceramics artist Steve Degenhart; the bison artwork is by photographer Audrey Hall.

LEFT: In a room with low ceilings and a lot of wood on the walls, West leaned into a darker palette, creating a cozy, layered feel with a vintage Indian block print throw on the bed and the dreamy panoramic wall covering, Au bord du lac by La Maison Pierre Frey, dominating one wall. The sofa is vintage, covered in a Pierre Frey embroidery.

171

West strove for an open feeling in the primary bath to create a spa-like ambience. The wall and floor tiles were handmade in Morocco by Zia Tile; the custom vanity is travertine. Pierre Frey's Tamanrasset linen drapery conceals the shelving.

As a homeowner and a designer, West is constantly evolving the house and grounds. In early summer, the landscape around the home is vivid and lush with views down to the river and across to faraway mountains. "At my core," she says, "I like a house full of friends, family, kids, and al fresco meals. I tried to create different areas for this: breakfast under the willow tree, cocktail hour on the sofas, afternoon reading naps in the hammocks, and, for cool evenings and après-ski relaxation, a sauna."

SAVING A
SEMINAL ICON

SAVING A
SEMINAL ICON

Across the vast open lands of the West, grain elevators stand as distinctive landmarks of the plains. Since the heyday of their construction in the 1920s and '30s, these "prairie skyscrapers," with their distinctive tall, shouldered silhouettes or more industrial cylindrical shapes, have bestowed gravitas on their towns and stood as beacons signaling from afar the location of the next settlement for road-weary travelers. But grain elevators—once symbols of prosperity and monuments to the industry of those who homesteaded the region—are disappearing all over rural America. They are torn down because they're unstable, the land beneath them is valuable, and their highly sought-after reclaimed lumber is stripped and sold off to enhance new structures with rustic accents. As many as 30,000 of these distinctive silhouettes dotted America's agricultural landscape in the 1930s. Fewer than a third remain standing today.

Visually dominated by its two historic grain elevators, Livingston, Montana, has always honored its identity as a railroad town. The tracks run along the edge of the town, across the street from its elegant historic hotel and busy eateries popular with locals and tourists. This is a town that has embraced its workaday side while resisting gentrification. It has retained its soul—even as the wonders of Paradise Valley's scenery, its proximity to Yellowstone, and its promise of both solitude and community have drawn musicians, artists, writers, Hollywood creatives, tourists, road-trippers, and second homeowners into its fold.

It was no surprise, then, that when longtime residents found out that their grain elevators were in danger of being torn down, they leapt into action. The Teslow, a 1906 landmark, towers over downtown, its bold, block-painted letters spelling out "Grain-Feed-Seed-Hay," serving as a reminder of the industries that built this community. But when high winds ripped the roof off, its demise seemed imminent. A grassroots group quickly formed a nonprofit and raised the money to purchase it. The Teslow will become an educational and arts center, preserving the town's character, history, and sense of community.

Yellowstone Granary, the tallest structure in town at eighty feet, was also in danger of demolition; its site had become a prime contender for redevelopment in a town that's seen a rapidly increasing demand for housing. Four locals—builder Chris Salacinski, architect Jordan Zignego, Brennan Ryan, and Kevin Muller—embraced the idea of adaptive reuse for the former grain elevator and flour mill. They would save the historic structure, rebuild it to last for at least another 100 years, and create seventeen units of housing. Zignego, assistant professor of architecture and director of Montana State University's Community Design Center, notes the challenges inherent in rehabilitating a century-old building whose central portion rests on a construction of stacked timbers with overlapping corners and is comprised of grain cribs and conveyor systems. "It would have been far less expensive to tear down the structure and build something new, but we wanted to honor this 100-year-old landmark that was important to the community," he says. "This made the construction complex and highly detailed, with very specific design constraints, but the result was worth it. This was a collaboration, and without the city of Livingston and the support of the community, it would not have been possible."

"These buildings are modern-day ruins and have transcended to the sacred. They're rural cathedrals."

For three years, Lindsey Thornburg had been assiduously scanning online rentals in Livingston when a new listing surfaced. A third-generation Montanan, Thornburg had lived in the Pacific Northwest, Colorado, and southern California before establishing her business in New York. But Montana had always been her constant—the place her relatives lived and worked, the home of her summer memories, and an unending source of inspiration for her designs and the Western aesthetic they represent. The clothing designer's cloaks and coats, while handmade in New York City's Chinatown, reflect that connection through her decade-plus collaboration with the legendary American company Pendleton Woolen Mills. "I've always loved Paradise Valley," she says. "There's a lot of energy there for really productive artists from the Western world; there's always been a profound Western narrative and really significant art coming out of Paradise Valley. Livingston is a nitty-gritty small town with a lot of love and intention within its fabric, and it's still financially attainable for most. It grabs the attention of an interesting range of humans."

As soon as she read about apartments in the Yellowstone Granary, she toured the building and was the first to commit to renting. "I fell in love with the project. It's like living in a piece of history. The walls are two-by-fours stacked on top of each other, and because it was an elevator, the grain was going up and down and eroded the walls away, so it has this depth, like carvings. The walls have this history and art within them. And I was so aligned with what the owners are doing. They were so passionate about the history and about bringing this structure back to life."

Thornburg committed to a two-story apartment for her living space and the top of the grain elevator for her office. The rooms of her apartment are imbued with warmth, texture, and a palpable sense of history from the wood cribbing, some sections deeply scoured from the passage of grain along the walls. The developers chose to leave the pipes exposed along the ceilings, creating a dynamic contrast with the expansive views over the town and rail yard and north to the Crazy Mountains.

Partly in deference to the visual impact of the scenery, Thornburg's approach to design has been one of restraint with a long-term view; she is taking a minimalist approach, which allows her to build layers over time in a fully-fledged expression of her Montana persona. From a patinaed copper vanity made by Bozeman artisan T. Lamar, to found stools, to a small painting by C. M. Okerwall of a rodeo clown, each item is imbued with meaning and holds significant personal value. Modern mixes comfortably with vintage, handcrafted, and found items. An early rare Pendleton blanket rests atop her bed, while 1970s modernist "paperclip" stools from Hugh Hamilton and Philip Salmon tuck under the kitchen counter. "My aesthetic is like Parisian flea market meets psychedelic western," she laughs. "Oddly, they all play into each other very well."

As Zignego puts it, "These buildings are modern-day ruins and have transcended to the sacred. They're rural cathedrals. You can see the original nails they pounded into the building; you can see the holes; you can feel the history."

The tallest structure in Livingston, Montana, the Yellowstone Granary has for a century served as a crucial landmark and source of identity for the town. When the community heard it was in danger of being razed, a group of preservation-minded locals committed to a bold plan of adaptive reuse for the former grain elevator and flour mill. Says architect Jordan Zignego, "My dream was to start with one material and only choose more materials when you have to. It's about that restraint and, I think, a back-to-the-land ethic. If you use fewer materials, the materials have to speak louder."

OPPOSITE: Minimal furnishings in the bedroom—a vintage Pendleton blanket by artist George Hunt Jr., an Electric Love feather sculpture, and a Flos light atop a vintage stool—allow the walls to speak.

ABOVE: Modern meets rustic in the bathroom: the shower stools were purchased at the MOMA store in New York.

Thornburg's atelier is a light-filled aerie. The large open space has windows on three sides to take in sweeping views of the town, rail yard, and the Crazy Mountains on one side and the peaks of the Absaroka-Beartooth Wilderness on the other. In Montana, Thornburg says, she enjoys a "spacious mental clarity" that she doesn't experience in New York. "It allows me to move slower and look at things from a less complicated mind. My focus is much clearer." Her designs hang on custom racks from LaMar Metalwork. The desks, pulled right up to the views, are also from LaMar Metalwork.

LINDSEY THORNBURG

LINDSEY THORNBURG

LINDSEY THORNBURG

MID-CENTURY
SANTA FE

MID-CENTURY SANTA FE

It is natural to think of New Mexico in terms of its art: sweeping landscapes featuring the Sangre de Cristo range, quiet depictions of pueblo life, the flowers and bleached bones of a Georgia O'Keeffe artwork, like her iconic paintings of skulls set against a backdrop of mountains and sky. But whether the piece depicts a grand vista, a Native ceremony, or a wood-laden burro, the sky, or the light washing from it, always comprises an essential element of Santa Fe works of art.

"New Mexico is very sky-focused," explains Santa Fe designer Stephanie Sandston of Greathouse Workroom. That focus may seem obvious, given the region's vast, cinematic landscapes, so often crowned by dramatic storms or cloudscapes. Where it's less obvious is in neighborhoods where homes are tightly clustered and where people are pursuing their twenty-first-century lives.

How to express that connection was a key concern for Allen Stamm, who practiced architecture in Santa Fe from 1939 until his death at age ninety-one. Even as Stamm developed whole neighborhoods, even as he kept his focus on affordable housing and everyday practicalities for the city's growing workforce in the thousands of homes he built, he never lost sight of the importance of the sky and the uniqueness of New Mexico's signature design characteristics and culture. He imbued his low-slung, earth-toned homes with the hallmarks of Santa Fe style: pine vigas, portals, and kiva-style corner fireplaces. At the same time, he designed with a forward-looking attitude and generosity of spirit that helped define the Santa Fe lifestyle and fuel its growth as a distinctive and historic small city, one that would be both sophisticated and family-friendly in the prosperous post-war era.

Evoking the connection to Santa Fe's landscape, culture, and history remains a key focus for interior designer Stephanie Sandston today as she crafts environments for her clients. Her goal, she says, is to "share the history of the layers of New Mexico." Sandston found that Stamm's vision of home provides the perfect backdrop to create a family retreat that reflects a sophisticated, modern New Mexico—a home that's imbued with an extraordinary level of thoughtfully curated detail in art and artifacts of the region, including custom pieces designed specifically for the project.

When a California-based couple who had been vacationing in Santa Fe for years decided to create a gathering place for their extended family, they sought an existing home that could meet their needs, provide flexibility, and function as a rental property when they weren't using it. It was important for the family that the home be modern, sophisticated, and fun while highlighting the art and artifacts of New Mexico; it would be their way of sharing an authentic Santa Fe with friends and family. The clients had known Sandston for years and had even rented a home from her in her previous life as a designer in Montana. The easy familiarity the trio enjoyed eased the stress of the new project for them all. And because the designer already understood the family's needs, preferences, and aesthetics, she says, she could focus on creating a home that was unique, highly flexible, and beautifully curated with special moments.

"My clients are especially trusting of my design process as we'd had the pleasure of working well together before," she says. "And I already had a head start because I knew what they loved and their leanings. They knew I'd consider their kids and their ages, the celebrations they were going to have [and the way they live]. That's what's really generous about this house: they're creating for their family but will also share it with others who are coming for an experience of Santa Fe. Those visitors will get a look at New Mexico with historical and current Native American pieces, current artists and artists from the '20s and '30s, and classic furniture design that is still very comfortable. Santa Fe is so drenched in history and experience; we're just rounding out their experience of a place and their history in this place."

Located in a historic residential area a short bike ride from the Santa Fe Plaza, the house was evolving just as the architect had intended it, explains Sandston. "Stamm was famous for his modernization of the New Mexican home. He was trying to provide high-quality affordable homes with really thoughtful New Mexican details in this new modernist architecture." One hallmark of his designs was the garage, designed to be turned into a casita or additional bedroom as a house grew with its owners. At some point an architect had done just that to this house; a second modest renovation had followed. In both cases the designers had remained true to the original intention, resulting in a thoughtful, warm, and welcoming home. In keeping with that ethos, Sandston's big architectural moves were minimal, allowing her to focus on the lived experience and careful curation of the interiors. "I wanted everything to be multifunctional and comfortable but sophisticated at the same time," she explains. "And the house needed to be flexible to work well for all family and friends, from children to family elders."

A combination of wood, stucco, and rusted metal creates a neutral but textured backdrop for rooms invested with a New Mexico modernist aesthetic, seen in a hand-picked collection of artworks, artifacts, books, furniture, textiles, and colors. In the living room, Sandston combined a set of mid-century Danish sofas with a steel-and-leather coffee table, a Nakashima-inspired walnut bench, a 1920s Pueblo dance painting, vintage pot shards, and a 1930s Navajo textile. This aesthetic continues throughout the house with vintage Native American beaded items, works by Georgia O'Keeffe and other New Mexican artists, vintage floating Danish case goods, and daybeds with custom Pendleton wool cushions.

Designed to sleep ten, the house can accommodate twelve—incorporating a fourteen-foot-long sofa, rollaway cots, and beds that convert from twin to king. Sandston furnished one room as a study that could flex as a second workspace, accommodate overflow sleeping, or host a poker game. A fourth bedroom was turned into a bunk room. She describes the kitchen as "workable," with seating at the counter and by the fireplace, which is useful during work hours and, once the computers have been put away for the day, offers a nice space at cocktail time.

Sandston built on Stamm's understanding of the importance of light—as did one of the subsequent architects who added a bank of clerestory windows. This home has views to the mountains with floor-to-ceiling glazing in places, windows in the bunk room, and an indoor-outdoor flow on both sides of the home, including a walled courtyard at the entry that creates additional outdoor space. A patio with an outdoor kitchen, firepit, and a table large enough for Thanksgiving gatherings dramatically expands the space and allows for four-season living under that ever-present sky.

Sandston felt lucky to work on a vintage house, and to build on Stamm's ideas about how to live in New Mexico in a modern but regionally specific way. "The house did what it was meant to do, which was to change and grow with the next generation," she says. "It already had a generous spirit, and the original vision provided by Stamm and his craftsman has been carried on with each new family and each designer who has had the honor to contribute to this home."

A mid-century-modern adobe by Santa Fe architect Allen Stamm was sensitively refreshed by designer Stephanie Sandston of Greathouse Workroom. For a California couple who'd been vacationing in New Mexico for years, Sandston layered regional items, references, textures, and colors throughout every room in the house. In the dining area, she grouped a reproduction 1913 Marsden Hartley painting, (*Berlin*), a mid-century tulip table, and reproduction Paul McCobb lacquer dining chairs from CB2. Sandston's Greathouse Workroom designed the banco, which is accessorized with Bauhaus-inspired custom pillows from Lisa Jensen-Nye. The bread bowl from Box Road Antiques dates from the 1800s.

LEFT: A sleek, highly efficient stove adds a sculptural element and keeps the room toasty without taking up too much room. A circa 1920s Shiprock, Santa Fe, Navajo natural rug occupies pride of place.

Sandston found the leather-and-steel bench at Garza Marfa. The small India ink artwork *Ocmulgee Mound* by Daniel McCoy was purchased from Hecho a Mano gallery in Santa Fe.

ABOVE: At the breakfast bar: walnut stools from Industry West and a colorful Georgia O'Keeffe print.

PRECEDING OVERLEAF, LEFT: A cheerful red Eames table provides a pop of color in the cozy study. The assembled banco with custom Pendleton blanket cushions was a collaboration between Greathouse Workroom and Lisa Jensen-Nye.

PRECEDING OVERLEAF, RIGHT: A garden suite for guests looks out onto a sunny private patio.

RIGHT: The primary suite highlights India ink on paper artworks by Daniel McCoy: *Spirits in the Sky* and *Spirits and River*, both from Hecho a Mano gallery. The Oklahoma-born artist trained at the Institute of American Indian Arts in Santa Fe.

OPPOSITE: Soft desert colors and regional references combine in a guest bedroom with a Pendleton blanket and a Georgia O'Keeffe reproduction painting from the Georgia O'Keeffe Museum in Santa Fe.

LEFT: The red steel patio set from Hay adds a touch of color to the private patio; the classic butterfly chair adds a bit of history.

URBAN HOMESTEAD

URBAN HOMESTEAD

Seeing the last child off to college often triggers a life reassessment. For a Colorado couple who had spent twenty years on a working ranch, becoming empty nesters left them imagining life in town. After touring the region's small cities, they focused on Bozeman—they were sold on everything from its amenities, lifestyle, community, and outdoor opportunities to the accessibility of its airport. Then, they made an unexpected move. Rather than buying in an established neighborhood or in a new development outside of town, they purchased a corner lot in a semi-industrial neighborhood with an edge-of-the-railroad-tracks vibe. Near the old shipping and receiving depot are vintage bungalows, new art galleries, quiet dead-end lanes, and a recording studio and music venue bringing a funky, youthful vibrancy—all within walking distance of Bozeman's bustling downtown.

Erik Nelson of Thinktank Design Group was tasked with designing a house that would be modern in its aesthetic while sensitive to the history and ethos of this evolving mixed-use neighborhood. The first goal was to avoid overwhelming its surroundings. "In terms of integrating, whether in town or on thousands of acres of ground that has never been touched, there should always be a respect for place," he explains. "For this project, we did tons of analysis looking at massing, relationships to other buildings, sun angles, and all the other things that create a thoughtful approach to how we're going to build."

The shotgun-shaped lot called for a structure whose long axis would run north-south. To mimic the scale and size of a smaller home, the house is conceived as two main volumes with corresponding rooftops. The architect added secondary spaces while keeping the larger forms of the house distinct. Creating separations within the building offered opportunities to bring natural light into the interior spaces—crucial during the long Montana winters. The house presents with steel beams, textural cedar siding, an interplay of metal-capped wood rafters over an entrance porch that has integrated firewood storage, and board-formed concrete with a standing-seam metal roof. Rot-resistant Accoya wood is used on the ends of the main gabled forms. Says the architect, "So much in the architecture and materials evokes a world made by hand. For the cedar siding, the idea was to find a type of wood, appropriate to the scale of a neighborhood but evoking the mountains. We used rough-sawn cedar cut at various widths and stacked, almost like stacked crib construction."

The three-story home lays out over five levels, with each living area given distinct character while still feeling connected to adjacent spaces. The interiors reflect the integration of contemporary design elements, such as steel applied on volumes that help define the home's interior flow, with organic materials like wood accents on ceilings and rafters, flawlessly executed by North Fork Builders. Recessed trim, indoor-to-outdoor staircases, a second-floor deck overlooking a living roof, and multi-material accent walls add interest without distraction—which was helpful in incorporating the owners' extensive collection of art, antiques, and objects.

Designer Susie Hoffmann of Envi Interior Design Studio was tasked with melding the architecture such meaningful items as heritage pieces from the wife's Swiss family. "We faced the challenge of taking the somewhat contemporary envelope, bringing in

"In terms of integrating, whether in town
or on thousands of acres on ground
that has never been touched, there
should always be a respect for place."

antiques, then buying and designing new furniture that would tie everything together," she says. "It was a lot of fun; we don't often have clients with heirloom pieces. To some degree, we had to be selective about what we could use. It also gave us opportunities to get really creative. We took a small armoire and turned it into the powder-room vanity. In the dining area, we hung an ornate gilded-framed painting of a naked woman lounging—something you wouldn't expect to see on a board-formed concrete wall. The mid-century-style furniture includes bold, emerald green chairs. The end result is eclectic and unusual, but everything works well together."

The result of this intriguing challenge is a project that sings with unique flair. "It was an exercise in getting to know the clients and their styles and bringing all these elements together in a collective and cohesive way," says Hoffmann. To do that for a couple making such a monumental lifestyle move made it all the more compelling. "A lot of people move to Montana to get away and to be in the wilderness. For this couple, it was the opposite. It was an exciting new venture to be a part of a community and to experience life in town."

For a Colorado couple searching for a new frontier, an in-town home in Bozeman, Montana, proved the most interesting opportunity, one where they could carve out a new way of living while creating a home for their most meaningful art and objects. The project, by Thinktank's Erik Nelson, North Fork Builders, and Susie Hoffmann of Envi Interior Design Studio, lives large over five different levels with a strong connection to the outdoors despite the urban setting. The light-filled kitchen features walnut cabinetry, Taj Mahal countertops, and a backsplash of Ann Sacks Savoy ribbed tile. The Roll & Hill light fixture and Miniforms barstools were chosen for their minimal profiles.

PRECEDING OVERLEAF: In a living room filled with rich hues, the designers selected Lawson-Fenning lounge chairs, a Verellen sofa, a glass side table and lamp from Miniforms, and an antique chair reupholstered in Morris & Co. fabric. The ottoman and pillows are custom; the antique artwork is from the clients' collection.

OPPOSITE: Arranging the house over multiple partial levels created interstitial spaces for work or meditations. In the sunroom, a Baxter chaise, vintage rug, and Casamance drapery fabric create the perfect setting to curl up with a book.

LEFT: Lively Pierre Frey wallpaper in the primary bedroom injects energy into a quiet retreat space. The custom bed by Green Seam Designs is covered in Casamance fabric. The bedside sconces are from Allied Maker.

Onyx Tile's Cinder Gray Raked Stone tile creates a serene backdrop for ablutions. The sconce is from Jonathan Browning; the chandelier is vintage.

TEAMS

SHOULDER SEASON

Architecture: JLF Architects
Interior Design: Debra McQuin and Robyn Seldin
Construction: Big-D Signature
Landscape Architecture: Verdone
    Landscape Architects

WHITE SNOW, BLACK DIAMONDS

Architecture: Locati Architects
Interior Design: John Vancheri Interior Design
Construction: Schlauch Bottcher Construction
Landscape Architecture: Design 5
    Landscape Architecture

WYOMING BASE CAMP

Architecture: CLB Architects
Interior Design: CLB Interiors
Construction: Capstone Construction
Landscape Architecture: Agrostis, Inc.

OFF-PISTE SUN VALLEY

Architecture: Peter Zimmerman
Interior Design: Barbara Gisel Design
Construction: Lee Gilman Builders
Landscape Architecture: BYLA Landscape Architects

MOUNTAIN MODERN

Architecture: Pearson Design Group
Interior Design: Alice Cramer Interiors
Construction: OSM Construction
Landscape Architecture: Field Studio
    Landscape Architects

FRAMING THE LANDSCAPE

Architecture: Studio Architects, Van Bryan
Interior Design: Hetherington Interiors,
    Abby Hetherington
Construction: Schlauch Bottcher Construction
Landscape Architecture: Highridge Landscapes

MONTANA MINIMALIST

Architecture: Doug Minarik
Construction: Archer Construction

INDUSTRIAL FRAMEWORK

Architecture: Pearson Design Group
Interior Design: MC Design
Construction: OSM Construction
Landscape Architecture: Agrostis, Inc.

SOLACE IN THE TETONS

Architecture: Northworks Architecture
Interior Design: Rendezvous Design
Construction: Teton Heritage Builders
Landscape Architecture: Rendezvous Design

WRANGLING THE FAMILY

Architecture: JLF Architects
Interior Design: WRJ Design
Construction: Big-D Signature/Dovetail Construction
Landscape Architecture: Blake Nursery

ESCAPE TO THE LAKE

Architecture: Greg Matthews Studio
Interior Design: Urbaine Atelier
Construction: Lohss Construction

FRENCH BOHEMIA

Interior Design: Fiona West
Construction: Coyote Contracting

SAVING A SEMINAL ICON

Design Architect: Jordan Zignego
Architect of Record: N2 Architecture
Interior Design: Lindsey Thornburg
Construction: C&L Builders

MID-CENTURY SANTA FE

Original Architecture: Allen Stamm
Interior Design, Art & Artifact Curation:
    Stephanie Sandston
Custom Textiles: Lisa Jensen-Nye
Construction: Melvin Figueroa
Landscape Architecture: Jeanna Giennke

URBAN HOMESTEAD

Architecture: Erik Nelson, Thinktank
Interior Design: Envi Design
Construction: North Fork Builders
Landscape Architecture: Design 5
    Landscape Architecture

ACKNOWLEDGMENTS

The Mountain West has informed our work throughout our entire creative lives. We are awed and inspired by the landscapes, the wildlife, the natural phenomena, the seasons. We are equally inspired by those drawn to this part of the world—a resilient, creative, hardy bunch of individuals. We have been so lucky to work with so many talented and creative interpreters of the West over the course of our thirty-plus year careers, and we owe a huge debt of gratitude to them, especially those featured in this book, for their vision and commitment.

To all the architects, designers, builders, craftspeople, landscape architects and contractors, engineers, art consultants, and fine artists whose work we've included here: thank you for being willing to share your time and your craft. We are especially grateful to the homeowners who have welcomed us into these most sacred family spaces. From lake to ranch, from city center to mountaintop, each one is special, unique, and intentional.

We are ever thankful for our long relationship with Gibbs Smith, Publisher, and the extraordinary team this employee-owned company has assembled, and retained, over so many decades. To our longtime editor, Madge Baird (who just celebrated fifty years with the firm), you have been our rock. We have enjoyed working with editor Jennifer Adams, a much published author in her own right; we appreciate her heroic efforts and attention during a hectic time. We are so grateful for the teamwork of Suzanne Taylor, Michelle Branson, Kim Eddy, Michelle Bayuk, and the sales and marketing teams. To a one, they are incredibly hardworking, talented, and committed to creating the best books possible. To our book designer, Glen Volpe of DYAD, and to Ryan Thomann and the Gibbs Smith production design team, we can only say thank you for making our work look so good.

Architecture and interior shoots can be time-consuming and logistically complicated; they require a relentless quest for perfection. To Betsy Stevenson, Allie Louise, Ezra Olson, Guthrie Devine, Kristen Newbern, and Alex Simpson, your help on location—with logistics, styling, and assisting in every way to get 'er done—has made all the difference.

We had so much fun shooting portraits set against vintage rustic outbuildings in the shadow of the Tetons with Jackson photographer Lisa Flood. She has a singular ability to tell a story through photographs; she managed to capture the essence of our long friendship and working partnership in one laugh-filled session in a place we strive to honor through our work.

We couldn't do the work without our emotional and physical support teams, especially those who house and feed us on our road trips through the mountain states. Deb Stegelman, Ann Simpson, Sue Simpson Gallagher, Beccy and David Billings, Sandy and Paul Zuber, Lisa Diekmann, and Carter and Ellie Reynolds have generously opened their doors to these wandering waifs and for that—and, more importantly, for the sustaining friendships—we are beyond grateful.

Audrey's mom, Coco, cheered her on every step of the way. Suzie, Jeff, Finn Hungerford and Sara Andrews cared for "Ollie" while Audrey was away on photo shoots. Thank you to Alison Merritt for her support of our books and artistic and musical endeavors at the Western Design Conference every year.

We'd like to thank our husbands, Todd Harris and Charles Ewald, and Chase's daughters, Addie, Jessie, Ross, and Katherine, for making it all worthwhile. Spending time with them in the Modern West brings the work alive. Finally, we'd like to thank each other for an amazing, inspiring, happy, and productive working relationship and friendship. It has lasted almost twenty years so far and the inspiring ideas keep coming! People always ask how and when we met; while we can't pin down a date, we know it was born of our shared love of the Mountain West. It's a place that captured our love early in life. The goal of our work is to honor that.

ABOUT THE AUTHOR AND PHOTOGRAPHER

CHASE REYNOLDS EWALD fell in love with the American West at age ten, the moment she first rode a horse through Wyoming sagebrush.

Since then she has been chronicling the West, authoring nearly twenty books including *Wild Sugar* with artisan baker Lindsey Johnson and *At Home in the Wine Country* and *California Coastal* with coauthor Heather Sandy Hebert. *Modern West* is her seventh work with Montana photographer Audrey Hall. Their previous collaborations include *American Rustic, Cabin Style, Rustic Modern,* and multi-award-winning *Bison: Portrait of an Icon.*

A graduate of Yale and UC Berkeley's Graduate School of Journalism, Chase is a freelance writer, editor, and consultant who helps creatives craft their stories. She lives with her husband and four daughters in northern California and embarks on road trips around the mountain states whenever possible.

Rooted in the dirt of the American West, **AUDREY HALL** is an internationally exhibited and collected visual artist with a dozen design books to her name. She brings the rigor of her fine arts background to the challenges of creativity, resulting in a growing collection of publications, images, films, and fine art installations.

Hall is known for her poignant landscapes, ethereal equine abstracts, and intricate gold bison photographs. Her work is part of the *TIA Collection,* a distinguished private collection whose unique purpose is the lending of significant works of art to museums and institutions. Her latest series and book, *BISON: Portrait of an Icon,* won a National Outdoor Book Award and a Pub West Silver award, and was a Reading the West finalist, Foreword Indies Award finalist, and a High Plains Book Award winner for Art and Photography.

Along with longtime collaborator, Chase Reynolds Ewald, Hall has returned to the shelter genre to add their fourth book, *Modern West,* to their design suite.

For Charles, my partner in life and in the West,

and for Addie, Jessie, Ross, and Katherine,

women of the modern West.

— C.R.E.

For Coco, my loving mother. Artist. Trailblazer.

Modern before it was cool.

— A.H.

First Edition
29 28 27 26 25   5 4 3 2 1

Text © 2025 Chase Ewald Reynolds
Photographs © 2025 Audrey Hall

Published by
Gibbs Smith
570 N. Sportsplex Drive
Kaysville, Utah 84037

1.800.835.4993 orders
www.gibbs-smith.com

Designed by DYAD
Printed and bound in China

This product is made of FSC®-certified and other controlled material.

MIX
Paper | Supporting
responsible forestry
FSC FSC® C208677
www.fsc.org

Library of Congress Control Number: 2024951606
ISBN: 978-1-4236-6766-7